DS
527.9
.M5
1979

Mi Mi Khaing, Daw.

Burmese family

BURMESE FAMILY

AMS PRESS

NEW YORK

Illustrated by E. G. N. KINCH

Indiana University Press / BLOOMINGTON & LONDON

BURMESE FAMILY

MI MI KHAING

Library of Congress Cataloging in Publication Data

Mi Mi Khaing, Daw.
  Burmese family.

  Reprint of the ed. published by Indiana University
Press, Bloomington.
  1. Burma—Social life and customs. 2. Mi Mi Khaing,
Daw. 3. Women—Burma—Biography. I. Title.
[DS527.9.M5   1979]   959.1   76-6607
ISBN 0-404-15291-0

First AMS edition published in 1979.

Reprinted from the edition of 1962, Bloomington. [Trim size
has been slightly altered in this edition. Original trim size:
15.5 × 23.5 cm. Text area of the original has been maintained.]

MANUFACTURED
IN THE UNITED STATES OF AMERICA

To my
Father and Mother
who in their daily living
have shown to five children
the shining path of moderation that is
The Middle Way

contents

introduction

THE FIRST time I met Mi Mi Khaing was, to me, a moment partly of delight and partly of embarrassment. My husband and I were traveling through Burma and a mutual friend in Rangoon had given us a letter of introduction to Mi Mi—but under her married name. Meanwhile, I had, of course, read *Burmese Family* because it was, at the time (and I dare say still is now), a "must" for anyone visiting Burma. Touring through the beautiful jade-green hills of the Shan States, we came to Taunggyi, the capital. An untidy-looking town, scattered over the side of a hill, but caught in beauty by the flowering trees—jacaranda that sheds a light as blue as snow, poinsettia that grows there in two varieties, a subtle parchment color and the usual scarlet, and then the incredible pink of cassia.

Inevitably, we called at once on Mi Mi and her husband, who was then chief education officer for the Shans. We met a delightful and thoughtful man, and his wife, who was beautiful to look at, retained a modest and interior manner which was contradicted by flashes of brilliant wit, sharp observation, and what, in the very nicest sense, I can only call sophistication. We, my husband

and I that is, were having the time of our lives, and in the course of conversation, I asked her, "Tell me, what do you think of this book I've just finished, *Burmese Family?*"

For a moment she looked astonished, and I thought she hadn't liked the book. "Well," she said, "it's fairly accurate, I think. I'm not sure it's very good."

"Oh," I said, disappointed, "it's so hard to get good books about Burma—and I thought this one was—"

Mi Mi's husband interrupted gently, to keep me from a *gaffe*. "My wife wrote it, you know."

"—wonderful!" I finished, unable to stop myself in midstream. And I meant it. It *is* wonderful, full of lights and sidelights, full of fun and information, full of a joyous and understanding knowledge of Burmese life. I was sad that Mi Mi never knew that the tribute, slight as it was, came from my heart, not from politeness.

The Burmese have many gifts. A magnificent sense of the theater, an enchanting sense of dance and music (the most stylish instruments that I have ever seen in an orchestra), a splendid sense of the ridiculous, a most appealing ease in their own way of life, which never asks to be liked or disliked by foreigners—the Burmese immigration quota to the United States is never filled. But one thing seems to be lacking in the Burmese heritage: there are few Burmese books that can be translated into English for the Western reader.

There are, of course, the religious treatises so necessary to a Buddhist upbringing. There are occasional monographs or government papers on economic and social problems. Most of the texts for the *pwes* (the great theatrical performances that last all night) are either learned orally and passed down from father to son, or are so filled with improvisation, cracks about the current political situation, local jokes, that there is no way of transcribing them. But Burmese novels translated into English? Burmese poetry? Short stories? Essays? There is very little in that field, and consequently *Burmese Family* is a very special contribution. It tells us not only what the upbringing, customs, jokes, habits, pleasures of being brought up in Burma are like. It also performs that other essential task of good literature. It tells you what it *felt* like to live through all these experiences.

Mi Mi, with her penetrating eye, with her wide experience in the West, with her wit and her wisdom, and—I consider this a high compliment—her true sentiment for her country and its ways, effortlessly crosses the barriers of ignorance and misconceptions. As effortlessly, she surmounts the hurdles of good writing.

One of the sad effects of colonialism in Asia was that all of us grew shy about our arts, and, possibly even worse, our eyes were turned to the West. When we thought of foreign travel, we thought of going to Europe. If your family could afford it you would be educated in Europe. If you could afford it after you were grown up, you thought of taking your vacations in the playgrounds of Europe. If you wanted to hear music or see dance, you looked for foreign orchestras or watched ballet.

After independence in most Asian countries there was a sudden, almost passionate return to their own ways and arts. There was one terrible lack. You could learn about your own country even if you had been educated exclusively in foreign schools and geared to a foreign system of living. But how could you learn about your Asian neighbors? As an Indian I know very well that, after years of familiarity with the West—starting with A is for Apple (a fruit I had never seen at the time I was in nursery school) and ending with a reasonable familiarity with Chaucer and Shakespeare—I was still entirely ignorant of my own heritage, literature, history, customs. After some time I was able to come to a reasonable familiarity with India's writers, painters, sculptors, and daily life, too. But where could I find out about my fellow Asians?

For me, it took two extensive tours, lasting a total of four years, to acquire even a surface familiarity with the continent to which I belong. Before that I used to ask myself, at regular intervals, "You can name five French or English kings, can you do the same for Burma? Thailand? Indonesia?" All fellow Asians, all deeply a part of my concern. I used to tell myself, "You can speak English, a smattering of school-girl French, but what Asian language besides your own can you talk in even a broken way?"

Certainly, my education at that time could be nothing but depressing in its answers. The only cure was to travel and see for myself. This was expensive, complicated, and not open to most people either foreign or Asian. I couldn't even find more than a few outdated books to instruct me on my way. Most of them were written by foreigners.

This, I realized, has been another curse of Asia. The vast mass of our travelers have been foreigners who ask for something quite different from what Asians ask of each other. People from abroad have, for centuries, traveled among us and written *about* us—writing, that is, from the stranger's point of view. We have kept a decorous, or sensible, or necessary (as you see it) silence about our own affairs and our own civilization.

Some people claim that the expressive energies of Asians were dissipated in the political activity to rid us all from European colonialism in our continent. Others claim that we have no talent for expressing ourselves anyway. Whatever the explanation may be, the body of literature about Asia by *Asians* is chillingly slender. I mean, specifically, books written from the inside to the outside world, as opposed to the (sometimes sympathetic, sometimes antagonistic, often romantic, almost always false) books written by the stranger gazing from some wholly foreign peak into a totally local situation.

Now, gradually, since the war, there has been a growing release of Asian talent in Asia and for the rest of the world. In this new area Mi Mi Khaing is a supremely welcome addition, partly because she gives us all such a short-cut to "understanding" (that quality that we are all urged to pursue in these internationally-conscious days), partly because there is so little material on Burma written by Burmese. Do you, for instance, know that Burmese women are independent enough to keep their maiden names even after their marriage? But that even though they can divorce their husbands simply by announcing their intentions to a few respected elders, they must still preserve their husbands' *hpon,* his maleness, "the glory or holiness of man"? Do you realize that a wife must never put her *longyi* (a kind of sarong) on her husband's bed or touch any of his possessions with her feet? How could you? There hasn't been anyone to tell you such intimate details about life in one of Asia's most important countries until, at last, Mi Mi Khaing spoke up about her *Burmese Family.*

Aside from her value as an accidental anthropologist for both Asians and Westerners, the real reason for the quality of her book is that she is a funny, expert, discerning and consistently interesting writer. She is also an enchanting person.

SANTHA RAMA RAU

September, 1961

preface to american edition

THE REPRINTING of a book such as *Burmese Family* fifteen years
after it was first written probably needs some comment which
will assess for the reader its relevance to the contemporary scene
among the people it describes.

These fifteen years have seen the resurrection of my country
as a new nation, at the same time as the forces of change have
most swiftly thrust into every stirring corner of the world. Surely
then, some of the life depicted in this book will have changed?

The independence which Burma won thirteen years ago did
indeed transform the spirit of its people. It gave them a new and
lively outlook. They had formed the poorer, the least venture-
some, the countrified element, in contrast to the ruling British and
other mercantile and urban residents: now they would control the
money, learn to make and use modern things, live in strength in
their own capital city, and fill its stage with Burmese activities.
Cloistered before from all foreign contacts except the governing
one, they would now exchange goods, services and courtesies
impartially with the whole world, while trying at home to fuse
the diverse smaller race-groups who still remained unfamiliar to

them after half a century of common British citizenship. They had been a people easily governed by an uncompromising paternalist rule: now they would hold rallies and make long speeches to reiterate that there should be no reservation of opportunity of privilege for any small group of people. A spirit of upheaval, of celebration and disorganization, and, naturally, of many disappointed ideals, replaces the old unruffled background. There is little security of life or prosperity guaranteed in such stirring times.

These are indeed great changes from the placid background against which *Burmese Family* was sketched. Yet I have heard visitors comment in surprise that so much written in the book is still true! It is a different Burma, with the same people.

In order to make this observation credible, I should, perhaps, try to explain why such big and rapid changes in the background of national life leave family and social life in Burma so little altered.

There are two respects in which traditional Burmese society has affinities with the spirit of modern times.

One is the position of Burmese women, who, having from early on in our history enjoyed equal civic and property rights with men, took modern equalities of opportunity as a matter of course. This meant that there was no great change in their position in the family or in society. The other point is that there has always been a near-equality in the living conditions of our "rich" and "poor," in that housing, style of meals, dress, and household effects vary as little as could possibly be expected with differences in the financial conditions of families.

Where tradition is to this extent in tune with current ideas, it is not likely to be thrown overboard. As modern life brought little that could make the Burmese women's lot more active than it had always been, for example, it was natural to retain their deference to the higher spiritual status of men, and the modesty expected of them in public. The national dress is a case in point. As it was already simple enough to allow easy movement, and followed the natural lines of the body sufficiently to suit modern taste, it has been retained, with extremely small concessions to international standards of fashion.

Though it is this stable position of Burmese women which has helped to keep society much the same, the other factor has contributed also. That near-equality in living conditions saved wealthier men's resources for a religio-social activity in which all classes could join with positive enjoyment. The feasting of monks and community which is described in the book is the prime expression of this. There has been no temptation to displace such a satisfactory system with imported and ready-made amusements. In fact, independence brought with it a livelier exercise of traditional activities, more and bigger feasts being given in the old style, or collections being taken to enable poorer men to give a communal one in their turn, because people felt they were now masters in their own house, led by a government which, from the Prime Minister downward, would be finding joy in these specially Burmese pursuits. And as this social life has elements of religion as its base, values such as the high place of monks and the attitude of reverence toward elders persist. The status goal continues to be identified with the spiritually satisfying goals of the son's novitiation and the monastery endowments, no less in present-day Burma than twenty years ago.

One strong feature of this book is the picture it gave of government officials' families. That surely should have disappeared, as a hated reminder of British rule. Certainly, the nomenclature has been deliberately changed, the idea of a privileged class has gone, the sacrosanct atmosphere altogether dispelled. Yet the essential feature of that life, the benefactor-dependent relationship, is still here. Our people, when deprived of cherished reverential submissions toward their exiled monarchy, gave tacit submissiveness and deference to the government set up by Britain; when that hand was withdrawn, with a great release of spirit as it were, they transferred deference elaborated and vociferated manifold, to ministers, new office-holders, or any citizens of importance who would carry on the traditional role of kind patron under a different name.

What has really vanished is the unquestioned sense of security and of the abiding nature of conditions under which we grew up. This is partly in line with changes over most of the world, but more because our country is particularly unsettled at the present time. Yet even in this respect, as we are volatile rather than deeply intense in our attitude toward life, any area of lull from dacoity and insurgent raids finds the untouched families still free from preoccupation with national cares, and still happy enough to enjoy their country-garden pleasures, while preparing in accustomed ways for a better and easier niche in the next existence.

MI MI KHAING

Taunggyi, Burma

BURMESE FAMILY

foreword

I WROTE this book in Delhi early in 1945 when Burma was still guarded by the Japanese invader. Its inspiration, therefore, was nostalgia and memories, instead of the surging life of my native environment which would have enabled these slight five thousand lines to carry with more strength the growth and the spirit of three generations in Burma. In offering the present result to readers outside Burma, I would have them be guided by the weighty verdict of my solemn friend U Thein Tin, who is known to the Burmese reading public as "The Dark Emerald" for the fanciful play of his pen. He returned me my manuscript with the words, "You have done what you can. It is for posterity to do better."

When a Burmese word is first introduced in the book it is printed in italics and thereafter in roman type. At the end of the book will be found a Glossary of such words, with page references to their first appearance in the text. A few proper names are included in the Glossary with page references to explanations which may help the reader.

chapter 1

*The village of Ye—my father's school days—my mother's
childhood home—my father studies in Moulmein, enters
government service, marries my mother*

Ye is a small Tenasserim town of great delight to Lower Burmans. Though the houses are congested, bazaars and cinemas
unknown, and robberies frequent and armed, the place contains
things very dear to all Burmese hearts. Good food to eat and
water to play with are found in abundance, amidst surroundings
which form a perfect background for an indolent holiday. The Ye
creek, muddy and about 50 yards wide at Ye, can be ascended to
chaung bya (stream's source), where there are gardens with bamboo huts and rich fruits on the trees surrounding, and clear swift

Tenasserim village

water for bathing; or descended to *pinlè wa* (ocean's opening),
where oysters and fat seafish are found and where there is a beach
with a pagoda on the first stretch of firm high ground and shells
along the foreshore. Now a train goes right up to Ye once a day
from Moulmein, and a motor boat can take you in two hours to
the gardens or the sea. My visiting cousins and sisters read Dee-
dok Magazines and English detective stories brought in their
luggage from Rangoon, as they lie on the bamboo platforms above
the water, but my grandmother and great aunts, who sit by talking, see the children only as reproductions of my father and his
brothers and sister, who were brought up here during the end of
the last century, without sight or sound of any world beyond the
two sides of the stream, the gardens and the sea.

Our stock is Mon, a race which came into Burma from Eastern
Tibet before the fifth century, by which time they had spread over
the Tenasserim coast, founding a kingdom at Thaton. They are
known as Talaings, perhaps because Indians from a place called
Telingana on the Madras coast came across with elements of
learning and religion, and infused their Dravidian blood into our
ancestors, so that even today Talaings are darker skinned than
their neighbor Shans and Karens.

My grandmother and grandfather spoke Talaing, a dialect distinct from Burmese, and had never been to any other part of
Burma; but Ye at the time my father was born (1880) had already
been under British administration for fifty-four years, and was not
very different from any other village of Lower Burma. There were
vague and grand stories of the metropolis of Moulmein and of
the growing far-off one of Rangoon and of exciting new fashions
and wealth that accompanied a knowledge of English and a job
under the government in the towns, but even my grandmother,
who, with her plot of paddy land and her fruit and vegetable
gardens, was among the wealthiest in the village, never connected
these with her children or those of her friends.

Grandfather died when quite young, leaving my *Paw-Pwa*
(grandmother) with four sons and two daughters, of whom my

father was the eldest. Like all the boys of the village, my father after eight or nine years of unrestrained childish delights when he could play all day, in the stream and up and down the village streets, stopping only when hungry or tired, wheedling the grown-ups to let him sit up till late at night listening to stories, was sent to the monastery on the outskirts of the village. The word for monastery in Burmese, *kyaung*, is the same as the word used for school, and it was to be taught learning and holiness, obedience and discipline, dexterity in manual and domestic tasks, and to be given a deep spiritual influence to last throughout life, that Grandmother and her friends sent their sons there. The parents whose hearts suffered too much at the thought of inflicting any punishment themselves now handed them over to the monks with the plea that they would teach them to be good and obedient, and chastise them severely if they did not obey.

The kyaung at Ye, like all kyaungs in Burma, was built in surroundings chosen for their pleasantness. On a slight slope overlooking the stream was a pagoda, the pagoda of the village where the people came on fasting and feast days to kneel on the paved platform around the tapering golden spire and recite the precepts. Down from the platform the steps were lined with shady trees, and to one side of this was the monastery, a wooden building with verandahs and tiered roofs, set in a large garden, containing a few flower beds for offerings at the altars, but chiefly wide shady spaces, great trees including a *nyaung-bin* (a sacred banyan, with huge spreading branches), flowering *gangaw* trees and deep green mango trees. In one corner was a well.

The monks consisted of the *saya-daw*, the senior monk who acted as head and abbot, about twenty monks who had been formally admitted to the order and were called *upasins*, and a number of novices who were wearing the yellow robe either for a short time, or to be admitted as monks later on. My father and his companions were admitted as *kyaungthas*, scholars. The monks spent their days in the recitation of religious formulæ and teachings, in meditation, in the telling of beads and the teaching of

scholars. They did this while observing a strict and simple life, abstaining from solid food after noon, possessing no goods except the essential articles laid down in the monastic rules, observing chastity and poverty. To the people of the village they were the embodiment of good and holiness, living the noblest and most meritorious life a man can live. The people addressed them in conversation as "Your holiness" and themselves as "Your holiness' pupil." The monks addressed the people as *daga*, giver, for they lived by the gifts of the people who donated robes, household articles and other necessities to the monasteries, as good works which brought them merit.

When my grandparents took my father to the kyaung he was a frightened little boy dressed in a cotton skirt called a *longyi,* and a shirt without cuffs and collar; his hair was grown long in the centre and tied in a knot, the sides being cut in a fringe about two inches long all round, and the rest shaved clean, a way of growing hair common to both little boys and girls and enhancing their youthful appearance. He and all the other scholars performed the domestic tasks of the monastery, swept and rubbed the good hard wooden floors, the monastery grounds and pagoda steps, because

in these precincts all comers went barefoot; they drew water for
drinking, and for the bath of the older monks; they followed the
monks on their rounds, two of them bearing a pole on which was
slung a covered tray, to take any food donated in excess of what
would go into the monk's bowl; they waited on the monks at
meals; they learned to read and write, and do simple sums, to
recite precepts and religious passages which they shouted at the
tops of their childish voices in imitation of the deep intoning
voice of the teacher monk, phrase by phrase; in the evenings they
went home to eat the meal which the monks abstained from, but
came back at sunset to recite the lessons of the day and many past
days all over again, to join in the assembled night prayers, to
sleep in the monastery and rise again before dawn.

When my father spoke to us of his years in the monastery he
always chuckled with delight, in spite of this long list of disciplined tasks. He had the advantage from the first; he was stronger
and taller than other boys, and in a system where all learning was
by heart he had brilliant memorizing powers. The school-room of
the kyaung had not the formal atmosphere of the Western school-
room with each child at a desk and chair, and a silence except
for the voice of teacher or child. The monastery boys all went
into the same big room of the monastery, irrespective of age or
stage, each with his slate or book, got down on the floor next to
their friends, crouched over their work and started to shout out
whatever passage was being committed to memory. My father's
chuckling was at being able to remember how his voice was
lustier than his rival's as he rested on his elbows and knees, and
rocked backwards and forwards in rhythm to his chanting, with
his legs going as high as he dared, giving surreptitious kicks and
nudges to upset the balance of his similarly rocking rival, shouting
out the passages all wrong when the supervising monk was at the
other end of the room, and could not distinguish his voice in the
general din, so as to cause his rival to laugh and be reprimanded.

But these shortcomings of the schoolroom were punished with
only a comical severity. During the play hour the lazy boys were

made to cross their hands across their breasts and pull at each ear with the fingers of the opposite hand; in this position they were made to sit and stand, sit and stand, while one of the good boys, usually joined by a crowd of others, sang in rhythmic chorus: "Hta-Htaing, Hta-Htaing: Rise-sit, rise-sit." Or if the supervising monk was in a playful mood he made these bad boys each take a good boy on his back and race them up and down the garden. Shortcomings of a moral nature were not regarded as such a joke, however; disobedience and dishonesty were punished with severe beatings, in accordance with the injunction given to the monks by the fond parents when they handed their children over: "So yin na na yaik pa: If he is naughty please beat him hard."

My father spent about five years like this. The hair of his top-knot grew longer year by year and it was nearing the time when he should cut it off, offer it to his mother as a tress for her hair-dressing, and have his head shaved and be initiated into the monkhood amidst feasting and rejoicing. This initiation, which every Buddhist boy went through in order to attain his true manhood by wearing the yellow robe, would last only a week or a month, or as long as my father felt the urge to remain in the monastery; forever if he liked, in which case he would be formally received as an upasin. It was expected, however, that he would leave after a few months and help Grandmother and the aunts with looking after the paddy and the gardens. A train of accidents upset all these schemes.

When my father was about fourteen he was already among the oldest boys in the kyaung, his learning was high and his conduct exemplary. The monks gave him the task of guarding the meat-safe where all the stores of sweetmeats given to the monastery were kept, as well as delicious titbits like the roe of nga-tha-lauk fish, and the rich red oil of the heads of lobsters, which were kept over for the meals of the monks on following days. These wire-netted cupboards are called "cat-houses" in Burmese, because they are meant to guard the food from depredations of cats, and they serve the purpose very well, but they could never guard against the appetites of little boys; for my father, even as I knew him in later years, loved people to eat good things and would always soften and allow his companions to have a bit just here and there. He was often scolded for it, but was so well-behaved otherwise that the post was not taken from him.

Just at this time, however, a supervising monk with very decided ideas of discipline was given charge of the boys; all the faults of disobedience, telling of falsehoods, running off to the village at forbidden hours and such like, were stored up till the end of the month. Then, on punishment day, the monk would gather a pile of sticks beside him, and all the boys with faults in a row before him, and go through beating them, one stick to one boy until it broke. One month my father was included in this row because the inroads on the meat-safe stores had increased in spite of constant warnings. Being a big boy he was left to the end of the row, and could watch the zealous monk methodically working through the boys and the sticks. What we know of my father and physical pain is that my mother was once scolded very severely the only time in her life that she beat any of us, and that he himself, when about to take nasty medicine or a vaccination, would go through a series of shiverings and comical protests, some of which I am sure were quite genuine. My poor father then watched the pile of sticks diminishing, and when there were but three sticks left and three boys between him and the untiring monk he suddenly took to his heels and fled, right out of the monastery grounds, down the pagoda hill and down to the creek. He did not dare to go home because Grandmother would have sent him back for a double beating, so he hitched up his longyi, tied his shirt round his head and swam across the stream.

One of the huts on the other bank belonged to a woman who had always been very fond of him because she believed him to be a reincarnation of her brother who had died in childhood; Burmese Buddhists believe that one goes through many existences on this earth, and sometimes children are born who have not yet forgotten their previous existence by the time they can talk; they adopt habits uncannily like those of the departed member, who, the fond and grieving relatives hope, has returned to them in the guise of this new child; they say "My bed," "My clothes" to the possessions of the dead person, especially if eggs are not included in their diet, the belief being that eggs cause them to forget. When we were very young, the fame of a wonder child, who could recite the most learned religious passages untaught, spread throughout Burma, and my parents travelled to hear him; he had been a monk in his past existence and could remember.

My father's case was no outstanding one like this; he had just resembled the lady's brother in looks and gesture, and a few childish utterances helped out by her belief had endeared my father to her as having been *winsa* (come into and inhabited) by her brother. The good and fond lady received the boy with open arms, agreed that he was getting too old for the monastery, and promised to go over and plead with my grandmother to take him out now and hasten his initiation ceremony into the priesthood. This was achieved and my father went back to his mother's house and prepared for the *shinbyu*, as the ceremony was called.

The manner of his exit from the monastery, however, had made him restless. During the short period he was free, he could go where he willed, and in this way he often met traders who came and went between Ye and Tavoy, a seaport town about 100 miles away, to which passenger and cargo ships from Moulmein made regular trips. One day he was at the house on the opposite bank when a boy he used to know as a toddler returned from Tavoy after a trip to Moulmein. This boy could speak a few words of English. Moreover, he wore his hair in a *boha-dauk* (a Westerner's crop) and seemed to think my father a jungle boy. All the restlessness in my father flowed over him, because up to now he had always felt himself clever and ahead of other boys. He worried Grandmother to let him go to Moulmein and learn English, and get a job with the government which would bring them hundreds of rupees each month. Other families who considered that

Grandmother had clever sons agreed that this would be a good idea; though none of them had been to Moulmein and my father was still a boy, it would not be so daring an adventure as it sounded, because there was someone among our relations in the village who had Anglo-Burman connections in Moulmein. These would put my father in school and look after him.

So after his shinbyu and his spell in the monastery, my father set off down the Ye creek to catch a sailing boat of trader friends who, in their sailing ships called *kattu,* ventured as far as the Nicobar Islands and could sail to Moulmein in about seven days. His head was now cropped, and my grandmother had put a ruby ring on his finger; he was sixteen years old, which was a very late age to start English schooling and pass it in time to get a good civil service job, but everyone at home thought he would do it easily for he had been the brightest boy in the monastery school.

Moulmein, Maul-la-Myaing to us, is a fair and prosperous city. It is fair in its descent from the hills behind, in three successive parallel main streets, to the wide Moulmein River, where seagoing ships can sail in, and an island rich in legend lies dark and green in the sunlit water. It had prospered since it was made the military headquarters of Tenasserim in the British annexation of 1826 until, in about 1900, it had over 50,000 inhabitants and a busy rice and teak export trade. Moulmein is fair also because the ridges behind are crowned with pagodas, and the hills and rivers contain waterfalls and caves, but to me it is particularly fair like a queen city that rides athwart her domain, because my father and my mother came from the two ends of the natural sphere of Moulmein's influence, Ye and Thaton, each from about 100 miles away, each sent by the family as an adventurous experiment, to meet and contract an understanding in Moulmein.

My maternal great-grandfather was a Talaing general, and when I look around at my mother's family I cannot think anything else; for they are all robust, alive and resurgent; whether I take the members who have chosen industry and renown, or those others who have concentrated on hard living and the en-

joyment of the pleasures of life, they all seem so ebullient, so much Lower Burman and not of the court of Mandalay.

My grandfather was a pleader by profession, but by reputation much more—he was a classical scholar famed for his fiery temper, his forthrightness and the stern discipline he imposed on all his children, grandchildren, dependents and anyone else who was given into his charge. He was also known for sudden progressive and even radical courses of action while expressing most reactionary views. My mother says he was a great man. My aunts loved to tell of his mental prowess, of how he never learned English, never spoke it, but always as he did his pleading in court he could understand everything that was said around him in English; my mother also told us of how beautiful he looked on a horse; and when he was playing *chinlon,* which is a light cane ball to be kept in the air by tossing with legs, shoulders, or any part of one's body that agility can devise, his short strong body, bare except for the longyi tucked about his loins, with tattoo marks in a blue-ringed pattern from waist to knee, and his long thick hair in a knot on the crown of his head, all looked more fair, more *manly* than the cropped hair, the shoes and socks and collars of the present punier generation.

Grandfather started his family in a village just outside Moulmein, but a fire burned down the house when my mother was still very young, and he decided to bring his family to Thaton and set up a practice there. He chose a site outside the town proper. It was then surrounded by muddy fields and, knowing Thaton at present with its 220 inches of rain a year, I can sympathize with my aunt Kyi-Kyi-Lon, who is said to have rolled herself on the ground with rage at beholding such a prospect.

The house which Grandfather built still stands today. There are not many houses left in Burma which reflect so well the type of comfort which a well-to-do family provided for in those days, or which have been built with so much regard to the customs of daily life and occasional festivities, and so little regard for appearance. Grandfather enclosed about three acres, big enough to have a road run through the garden for the general public to use at certain hours of the day. He sunk two wells, planted mango trees of the *dasu-may* (forgotten trees) variety for which Moulmein is famous, so delicious that a woman forgot her tresses in the ecstasy of its taste. The house always strikes me most as having no face; its shape followed the dispersal of its various functional units, and

Grandfather's house

each unit was placed on different levels from the ground according to the nobility or ignobility of the function that was to be assigned to it.

One of the wells was opened to the public use of the village as a good deed. The steps up were to washing platforms where Grandfather and the men of the family took their baths, and clothes were washed by the women of the house. From here three steps went up to a store-room and a long gallery which was mostly window and balustrade on one side. Here the family ate its meals and my aunts sat smoking their cheroots in the evening breeze. Three steps continued the verandah still higher to where the washing-faces water-pots and drinking water-pots were kept, and where morning ablutions were performed on to the water-loving *pein* (arum) bushes below. Right at the head of the verandah was a study room. From this high verandah two big steps went up into the main part of the house, which was two-storied, and which contained the altar at the head, on the east side. This was the body proper of the house, but a modern visitor would see no pleasant rooms here, for it was built for communal living and for grandeur of space on festival days. There was one room for Grandfather, and a movable screen formed a bedroom for my aunts, but the rest was a big noble open hall with round pillars of solid teak, twelve inches in diameter. Then from the back, other steps again led down to a part lower in function. A broad verandah contained at one end the birth chamber where the grandchildren were to be born, at the other, the powdering or dressing-room for my aunts. This verandah was definitely a female part of the house and nothing was under it except the stables. Under the main part of the house was a big hall

where Grandfather received his clients and, later on, my uncles and mother held a school for the children from the neighborhood. From the women's verandah a flight of steps led down to a big and airy kitchen with shady trees on one side and a vegetable garden on the other. Behind the kitchen were the latrines and a little bathroom for my aunts to bathe in private when they desired, with the water brought across from the well.

The house throughout was of the finest teak. In the main part the floor-boards were a foot wide and shining with the polishing of grandchildren's exercise. The windows had stout iron bars against the *dacoits* (robbers) for which Thaton was famous even in my day; the doorways from the verandahs had big folding doors, of six leaves, each doorway about eight feet wide and ten feet high, in memory of a nobler, bigger generation of Burmans, with three stout beams barricading it into position. The staircase closed with a trapdoor of solid teak.

This great household was run without any servants as we know them today. Grandfather brought up an Indian youth who was called Apana, in the way that a Welshman is thought of as Jones by English people, because my grandfather and some of my aunts refused to pronounce a true Indian name correctly. Apana looked after the horse for the carriage and carried water from the well. As grandchildren were born, they were sent back to be disciplined and educated after spending the first few years with their own parents. No child would have dared to withhold his offspring from the benefits of Grandfather's influence, until my father dared. There were ten members in my mother's family but the first five uncles and aunts are only legendary figures to me, for my

getting ready for school

mother was among the youngest and married late by Burmese standards, and my elder first cousins were of the age of uncles and aunts to us. There were ten of these cousins, born of three different families, sent back to Grandfather by the time the house reached its fullest and most pleasantly regulated stage.

In the early morning before dawn my aunts would get up and cook the rice, to offer it at the altar with sliced fruits, and say their prayers. They cooked the morning meal after this, with foods from the garden and from hawkers, women who came around with cane trays of fish, poultry, and vegetables on their heads. The meal was cooked by the time the procession of monks came through the road running across the garden; the various dishes were put into little bowls placed either in the monk's bowl or on the tray carried by two scholars behind. One of my aunts then rolled a low round table out of the store-room into the long verandah, laid a mat beside it and served Grandfather's meal.

In the meantime, another aunt saw to the children's preparations for school. She sat in the open doorway leading to the washing platform, with a comb and a bottle of coconut oil beside her, and the children came up to her one by one. Both girl and boy cousins had their hair done in the same way as my father's was when he went to the monastery. My aunt oiled each head, combed the long tresses out and knotted them; in front of the little girls' knots she stuck a small arched ivory comb and on festival days she arranged a circle of flowers in its place. Then the cousins raced each other down the steps and splashed and bathed at the well, the older ones drawing water for the younger. Up from their baths they put on clean school clothes, and sat around the low table after Grandfather had finished his meal. All the dishes were laid out for the older children to serve themselves, but the younger ones had their plates heaped with portions of everything. After eating, each child ran with his plate out to the washing platform and put it in a wooden tub ready for washing, washed his fingers and lips and came back to dry them on the common napkin. They were not encouraged to drink water during the

meal; they went up to the high verandah after it, where the water-pot was on a stand, with a ladle hanging from it—a smoothened coconut shell with a handle stuck through a hole in it. On the table beside it were the drinking mugs, of lacquer, smooth silver and carved silver work.

With the children gone to school, my aunts did all the household tasks, changed the water and flowers on the altar, washed clothes, rolled cheroots, pickled and preserved fruits and vegetables in dozens of big jars. When my cousins returned they were given an early dinner and sent down to play in the garden. My grandfather would go down and sit there and have one after another come to him to learn the scriptures. When it grew dark they came up and the elder ones read their lessons; the younger ones played at polishing the shining teak floor. At about 7:30 they were taken into the altar room to shout their prayers aloud.

These accounts of the childhood of all my elder cousins sounded most stern and disciplined when told us in our own pampered childhood by my gentle mother; she was with them at that time, still unmarried, the youngest and fairest daughter and the apple of Grandfather's eye; to my cousins, not a disciplining aunt but some one very near their own age, to her elder sisters a

sweet young girl, who was going to receive more book education than a domestic training like theirs. When I see my grown-up cousins, however, I cannot imagine any routine which their lively minds did not animate; their characters all bear a consistent stamp of push and cheerfulness and, far from their regimented years robbing them of anything, they have gained a kind of education which is rare in these days. Would that my father had not held such decided views on his right to indulge his children as he wished and had sent us for chastisement and learning in our religious teaching.

My grandfather at this time must have known a deep felicity of spirit as he sat in his garden in the evenings. Seated on his broad and stout chair, with a betel box and spittoon on one side of him, and his favorite and most learned grandchild, my cousin Lu Pe, now Superintendent of Archæology, reading the scriptures to him, he could sit in the shadow of his solid teak house, with a row of mango trees before him, the townspeople using his well of clean good water, the road through his garden which was open at the hottest hours of the day for all wayfarers and sellers to find a short and shady route across, his garden with flowers for altar and vegetables for kitchen, and stray trees which are an asset in any garden—the *gwe* tree whose fruits were sweeter and larger than the ordinary, the *dandalun* with pods to curry and leaves for soup, the *ywetyo* with its leprous looking fruit which are for the connoisseur and to be eaten as cure for coughs. How blessed for my grandfather at the end of his days to have attained such peaceful comfort and to feel that he had passed on religion, literature, discipline of mind and body to the generation of his grandchildren.

> To dwell in a pleasant spot, to have done good deeds in
> former births,
> To have set oneself in the right path,—this is the greatest
> blessing.
> Much learning and much science, and a discipline well
> learned,
> Yea, and a pleasant utterance,—this is the greatest blessing.

(From the *Mingala-thot-pyo:* Song of Blessing.)

My mother, as I have said, was the fair young jewel of her father's eye; and my grandfather had flashes of the most radical behavior. Though he refused to learn English and this irreligious language was never spoken in his house, he suddenly decided to send my mother to learn English, not just as a second language, nor even to spend a few years at a totally English-speaking school—for an accomplishment, as a few other Burmese girls of the time did—but to study seriously until she passed the High School Standard of a European Code school which did all its teaching in English. My mother was thus the first Burmese Buddhist woman to pass the High School Examination in the European Code, and today she can speak faultless English though she never uses it unless necessary, and can even read some of the books of Virginia Woolf, although she does not like them. She and her two young brothers were sent to Moulmein; they stayed at the house of my eldest uncle, who had settled there, and my mother attended an American Baptist Mission school. This was just before 1900.

My father, in the meantime, had arrived in Moulmein at the same time as my mother. The world had opened for him suddenly. After the strict and simple life of the monastery he found himself a smart young man with a Western crop and a collared shirt and outer jacket. He carefully put away his mother's ring to be put on again only on his visits back to Ye; he found a big and busy town to range in and no anxious mother waiting at home. I think it was during these years that my father got his love of all the sweet pleasures of life. A non-smoker and a teetotaller, he was one of the most spontaneously happy people. He loved food and many friends, to see young people happy and free from discipline, to spend all his resources in order to create happiness around him; he glorified the ability to think and work quickly and leave the maximum time for eating and laughing.

Particularly in this, Moulmein appealed to him. Having grown up in the monastic system of education by memorizing, he was bewildered at a system which prescribed a whole year of full-day studies for five or six thin text-books. As soon as he could read and understand he committed all his year's text-books to memory within a month, and could not conceive that there was anything else to be learned unless they prescribed fresh books to be memorized. During school hours he wrote an arithmetic book for an old man called Samuel who produced a series of swot books on various subjects, beautifully tabulated books with questions and answers, invaluable for examinations and used even in my day when we and our school teachers whisked them out of sight of Education Inspectors who came on the prowl for just such unprogressive methods of education. He also went across to the American Mission School, where quite often the teachers were more Christian and painstaking than brilliant, to help old Teacher Nellie with geometry riders, and in this way he met my my mother.

My parents could not get married as soon as they left school.

My father had first to go to the University, which consisted then of Rangoon College, affiliated to Calcutta University, and then he felt he must work to buy my grandmother a big enough plot of paddy land so that her two youngest sons would not need to look after her in Ye, but could come into the world like my father. He now felt that they should not be denied the wonderful opportunities which he had found. My father did go to College, but had passed only his F. A. (corresponding to Intermediate) when he heard that my mother was now going out to teach in a school at Thaton, and that she was having to put on a European gown and hat in order to be less conspicuous, because at that time no Burmese Buddhist ladies went out to work. My father left his studies at once and got a job in the same school to look after her, and it was only after some months of persuasion by Grandfather and my mother that he consented to leave and look for a better paid position.

He managed to obtain a myookship in the Government Service, which is a junior administrative post but considered a very good job for Burmans in those days. In this job he could save enough to buy Grandmother her paddy land, after which he and my mother would get married. But my father with his good looks, his teetotaller habits, and his myookship, was considered a desirable son-in-law by many people, and other parents were not like Grandfather; they would try to engage the young man's affections for their daughters. I am sure my mother spent the next three years in some anxiety, as she heard stories of the young myook's gay and happy life in such far-off towns as Toungoo and Shwegyin. But one day the children dashed up to her with a telegram; she opened it and read *Gyi will you marry me.* My mother, who has never shown any excitement as far as I can remember, got up very quietly and went to her chest of drawers. She took out ten annas in change, and wired back *Yes.*

Soon after this my father arrived amidst great excitement on the part of my mother's family and a pretense of complete ignorance on Grandfather's part. My aunts expected an explosion

Father and Mother become engaged

from him when my father went in to ask his permission to marry his most beloved daughter, because Grandfather liked tradition in all things, and traditionally my father's parents or other elders should have approached him first, but there was no explosion; the fierce old man said: "Maung Chit Khaing is a good man."

chapter 2

My childhood in a minkadaw *family—"upstairs girls"—household articles—Burmese crafts—imported goods*

By THE time that I was about four years old my father had become a Subdivisional Officer in the Civil Service, and our family had joined the ranks of what has now come to be known as the *minkadaw* class, an *a-so-ya min* being a government official and *minkadaw* the wife of a min. The minkadaws usually referred to were in the great majority the wives of officials of the Burma Civil Service, Class II, and by the time that we were passing through our childhood and adolescent years they already formed a very definite stratum in Burmese society. We children now comparing notes with the children of the minkadaws posted as far apart as Tavoy and Myitkyina can find common characteristics in all the households, from domestic commodities and meal habits to social conventions and standards of wealth. It is as though a new upper middle class has grown up, complete with

a government official's household

snobberies, in what was formerly a classless Burmese society, but a class that still keeps itself quite apart from the European gymkhana life of the district towns.

The houses which I can remember, when my father was a Sub-divisional Officer in the subdivisional towns of Zigon and Mya-naung, where he was in charge of the subdivision, or in the divisional headquarters town of Magwe, where the whole hier-archy of min from the Commissioner downwards were present, or in the district headquarters town of Maubin, where the min ranked down from the Deputy Commissioner and my father was Headquarters Assistant, all bore certain uniform features. They were all wooden, two-storied and large, with a sufficient number of big rooms to have a dining-room and an office room below, a sitting-room above the portico and two big bedrooms, besides little verandahs and odd rooms. They all had a front staircase for common use and one or two ladder-like staircases behind for watermen, sanitation and servants. The kitchen was about twenty yards away, connected by a covered passage, and at the back of the large garden or compound was the *tanya*, a row of rooms for men servants and Indian servants. The garden in front was usually modest owing to frequent changes of occupants, but a minimum amount of flowers for daily vases on the altar had always to be cultivated, and fruit trees were prized highly, guava, mango, marian or citron.

Unlike most Burmese households, we did not have any aunts or other relatives staying with us, but we had our full quota of domestic dependents in whose company we spent most of our childhood. Minkadaws divide their servants into "downstairs servants" and "upstairs servants." The downstairs variety are the usual domestics—cook, boy, gardener, office boy and so on. The upstairs variety are not referred to as "servants" (*a-say-khan*); they are girls whose work is all done in the rooms upstairs, who sleep there and spend the greatest part of their day in the quarters inhabited by the family. In many cases this system is one of abuse and oppression. The girls may be poor relatives—

cousins in the fourth degree perhaps—or they may be bought up from poor parents who, for a sum of Rs. 25 to Rs. 100 down and intermittent gratuities, will allow their children to go into a theoretically better home. These girls come at any age from seven to fourteen years. They are clothed and fed and their *mon-bo* (sweetmeat money) depends entirely on the mistress they chance upon. When they are young they play with the children of the house and when older they sweep and dust the upstairs rooms—rooms on which we walk only barefoot, as distinct from downstairs rooms swept by an Indian sweeper, and on which they use a feather broom instead of wielding a broom of coconut sticks, thus sealing the distinction; they also wash the personal garments of the household, look after the children and all other housemaid duties. They are rarely kept alone; there may be up to four or five according to the household.

The relationship with the family is that of feudal serf or poor relation. They do not call their employers *thakin* and *thakinma* (master and mistress); they address them as Aunt and Uncle-older-than-own-parents; they call the children of the family elder-brother or sister-so-and-so and address all relatives as the children do, but they have no definite salary, no rights and no external connections. It is only in rare cases, however, that girls reach the age of thirty in an environment not congenial to them; in ideal circumstances it is the duty of the mistress to settle them in an advantageous marriage by the time they are twenty-one or twenty-two. Failing this, the girls generally manage to elope, for elopements are frequent and not very scandalous in Burma.

In our childhood, when the family was big with growing children, we had five girls with us at one time. Of these, three were our relatives—two sisters, Ma Ohn Kyi and Ma Mya Shwe, who were third cousins of my father, and Ma Ngwe Yin, a second cousin of my mother. Both their families were far too poor to keep them. We had to pay respect to Ma Ohn Kyi and Ma Ngwe Yin, who were both a few years older than I and called us all by our names, but nobody stopped us from bullying the young

Mya Shwe and the two unrelated girls as much as we liked. A-Kyi, as we called Ma Ohn Kyi, was always treated as the senior one because my parents considered that she had a good moral character. She was fairly pretty, very quiet and reserved towards us, and enjoyed helping my mother with the babies, supervising the work of the servant girls and valeting my father. Ngwe Yin, who came to us as a very attractive girl with a reputation for being unmanageable even at a young age, always chose the task of taking us for walks in the evenings so that she could put on her nice clothes. She took us wherever she liked, or she sat with us at meal times and let us be as naughty as we wanted while she indulged in repartee with my father's clerks or chauffeur. Mya Shwe was my contemporary and playmate; she went to school while I was in boarding school but cut short her attendance the day I came home, irrespective of differences in our school calendars.

When A-Kyi was about nineteen it was announced to us that she was to be married to my father's clerk, Maung Hla Bu. This young man was a favorite of my parents and had been a constant admirer of A-Kyi, helping her to make the beds when my father took the whole family on tours, but awaiting the graciousness of my parents before he dared to ask for her in marriage. My mother gave A-Kyi a small trousseau and a few pieces of jewellery, and they were married shortly before my father got a posting to another station. When a child was born, Mya Shwe, who had outgrown her days as a playmate for me, went to stay with them. Ngwe Yin, the beautiful girl, continued discontentedly for about a year, and then she eloped with a student protégé of my father's. I don't think either of my parents were very shocked at this.

My memories of the girls who worked for us are happy enough, only because my mother had been brought up in Grandfather's house, where everyone was taught to do things for herself; in her character also was a pervading sense of tolerance. In some minkadaws' houses, however, I have seen two girls kneeling with soap and towel outstretched, while the mistress bathed herself. In more cheerful but no less aristocratic-minded households a meal laid ready on the table is the signal for one girl to get under the table and fan the mosquitoes off the legs of the family, and another to play the gramophone right through the meal. My gay young uncle San Lin extended the domestic duties of his girls to the learning of modern songs which he liked, and he did his morning dressing to the accompaniment of his servant girls with powder on their faces and jasmine buds in their hair, swinging their feather brooms to the rhythm of modern love songs.

A-Kyi and A-Shwe and all the girls we had before and after them bring back memories of the household articles which made with them a background never recovered in our later Rangoon days. My mother, like all minkadaws in the districts, did not depend on a big bazaar and shops to supply her with goods, but took a special pride in buying each product from the town where the best quality of it was manufactured. She could do this either by my father's being posted within its district, by going there on a pagoda-visiting expedition, or by having relatives posted there; and a survey of all the household possessions I can remember makes a cross-section of Burmese crafts. All our blankets were Burmese *saungs*, good stoutly woven cotton pieces, about seven feet long and four and a half feet wide. We had single ones of red, black and yellow stripes which looked very bright and barbaric; they came from the Chin Hills. We used these in the hotter months. During the colder months we used thicker *ok-saungs* which we got from Pakokku; they were fourteen feet long and used doubled, with a fringe at both ends. These were woven very strong and white, with bold red stripes on them in pleasing combinations. All these saungs washed more and more beautiful to our childish eyes. My mother had a big collection of them in wooden chests and some of them have lasted thirty years and are still beautiful.

She was also very jealous of her collection of *hpyas*, mats for sleeping or sitting on, woven closely of the fibres of a reed called

mats, pottery

thabaw, or, finer still, of the outer skin of a grass-like plant, the *thin*. These light and flexible mats or *thinbyu* came from Lay-myethna, "The Town of Four Faces." They were equally smooth on both sides and had velvet borders piped on, broad at one end and narrower at the other, to distinguish the head end for nobler use, and to be sure of always resting the feet on the same ignoble end. We had them in big sizes for the beds and for afternoon naps on the verandah, and smaller sizes for prayers and for visitors to sit on. My mother kept them in rolls, five or six rolled together according to quality, covered with a cylinder of ticking and stood end up along her dressing-room.

Although we used imported crockery for the table we could not do without Burmese pottery for other purposes. Water-pots and goblets of light pottery from Twante, near Rangoon, were necessary to keep the water cool. There must be special pots for the altar water, for washing faces, for drinking water (in which pot, however, we kept a sand filter bought from Rangoon), and goblets in all bedrooms. For baths we had big black voluminous jars from Upper Burma, of a less porous pottery with a salt glaze on it, about thirty inches high and wide-mouthed. Smaller ones like these were kept for pickling mangoes and other green fruits. In the kitchen also, the modern aluminum pots would not do for such purposes as cooking acid leaves and fish curry that had tamarind in it; an earthen pot was always used for *chimbaung*, roselle leaves. Moreover, the *salaungbon*, or cover, of an earthen pot can always be used for baking fish paste, a daily necessity, by pressing the paste flat on the inside of the cover and putting it over the fire; the top knob of the pottery always remains cool enough to be touched by the time the paste is baked. On festival days my mother bought dozens of little earthen dishes, no bigger than an English coffee saucer. They were called *hsi-mi-khwet*, oil-flame dishes, in which we burned lights of cotton wick and kerosene, and lined verandahs and window-sills with bright fairy lights in the night breeze.

We had stoneware in the house too. The *kyaukpyin* is a flat circular piece of stone for grinding the bark of the *thanakha* (*linnoria acidissima*) tree, to use as a cosmetic. It has a canal all around to receive the ground paste. Kyaukpyins can be bought in all varieties and sizes in any bazaar, but my mother always got hers through the headman of Salé village, in Upper Burma, where they use a particularly suitable kind of rock which is durable and yet helps to make the paste smooth. We had some beauties, heavy pieces of about fourteen inches across, a square around the circular canal, with carved figures on the corners and the ponderous legs. With the right quality of bark the ground thanakha fell in a smooth golden flow into the canal. Formerly, all women used this cream as the sole substitute for powder, letting it dry on the face to whiten it, but the sophisticated ones now use imported powder as giving a less artificial appearance.

Yet even the most ardent Max Factor fans cannot give up thanakha entirely, for its great value lies in its astringent properties; it would have great success with European women who use mud-packs, because it acts like a mild and pleasant mudpack. It also has cooling and refreshing properties. It is fragrant; older women apply it over the entire body after their baths, like talcum powder. My mother says it smooths the skin and, indeed, victims of smallpox who are left with deeply marked faces have their skins smeared with thick thanakha many times a day, and after a few months there is a definite improvement. The thanakha bark is the most used, but barks of the red and white sandalwood and other trees (*nethapyu, nethani, kalamè, a-hmway*) are more fragrant and are used on the body. Bad bark from the bazaar grinds gritty and dries patchily, but special consignments come from Myingyan and Pakokku, cut into six-inch lengths from branches two inches in diameter. A daily task of the girls in each household is to grind thanakha, and the commonest sight is a girl on a verandah with a kyaukpyin, a mug of water and a basket of logs; she pours water and grinds unceasingly, bored to tears, and then scoops the paste into separate dishes for use on face, body and legs.

combs, knives

Our toilet to this day has never included imported combs. Even the most frivolous girls in the University prefer Burmese combs. Burmese women, unlike Siamese and modern Chinese and Japanese women, wear their hair long without exception, and European combs could never cope with so much work. At one time, the village girls did favor long, bright bakelite combs to wind the hair around in a knot at the back, but the fashion was ridiculed as "aeroplane head-dress" and soon died. Burmese utility combs for general use and for distribution to servants of the household are made of wood and shaped according to use: for combing the hair are those with slightly curved rims, two inches wide and six inches long; for the little girls to stick in front of their knots and for women to form a frame for their formal hairdressing are small ones, almost semi-circular in the curve of the rim; for the women to wind their hair into a knot on less formal occasions are almost straight-backed combs; for delousing are fine double-edged combs. My mother chose wooden combs for smoothness and stoutness and put them at the bottom of the sesamum oil jar until the brittle yellow wood turned a deep rich brown. These combs, with teeth that bite and rarely break off, can be bought for three annas. We also had ivory and tortoiseshell combs for superior use.

Burmese blacksmiths have been busy since olden days, producing weapons for the hill people, agricultural implements, scissors, nutcrackers and fire-irons, and, above all, blades of all kinds (*dahs*). The dah is the universal implement in Burma. It serves as a fighting weapon in the form of a long *dalwè*, a slender pointed steel blade, about fifteen inches long, fixed by a tank into a long handle of cane or bamboo, iron-bound or tightly whipped to prevent splitting. In the form of a shorter dalwè, with or without a point, it is used as an all-round implement in housebuilding. With this bamboos are hewn, split open and slit into widths, boards of bamboo or planks are chopped for floorboards and timbers are hewn for posts. The short, broad-ended *dahmas* are used for heavy chopping and were the general choppers for meat and firewood in our kitchens. The dahma is a stout iron blade faced with steel. Lighter paring knives called *damauks* are also produced. Thus a Burman in a village normally carries a dah of some sort tucked into his waist as he sallies forth perhaps to find some firewood, housebuilding material or an enemy. The Shan people also had long murderous-looking dagger knives called *damyaungs*.

The iron-workers of Magwe sent us scissors which my mother preferred to stainless steel ones because they could be oiled and sharpened throughout a lifetime, and because they had inscribed on one blade her name and on the other "Health and wealth to you." We got our betel-nut crackers from there also; these had a blade on one arm, to cut as well as crack.

Our house, like every Burmese house, kept a betel box always ready for visitors. The box had a top tray with little cups or boxes for the chopped areca-nut, orange peel, spice seeds and lime, and a bottom compartment for fresh betel leaves of the betel vine (*piper betle*). A deep cover fitted the whole box. Grown-ups smeared lime on a leaf, wrapped nuts and spices in it and chewed it, spitting out the red juice, which is too strong to be swallowed. Betel has an astringent action in the mouth and by promoting the flow of salivary juices it aids digestion. Our betel boxes were of richly carved silver, with embossed designs of elephants, princes riding on horses in the forest, heavenly male and female spirits, all looking very alive. Silver carving is one of our show industries; the silversmiths at Mandalay and Moulmein produce handsome bowls, boxes, dagger handles and various other objects bought by foreigners.

Burmese people do not have the custom of buying *objets d'art* for their houses, but the articles of daily use which they like to have of good quality and pleasing designs are the real inspiration of these traditional crafts of Burma. The silver used ranges from rupee fineness up to the pure metal called *baw*. We had silver bowls, *ngway-balas*, of all sizes, smaller ones for drinking, bigger for pouring the bath-water, and enormous ones about twelve inches across for holding gifts to the monks on festival days. Sometimes my mother used these to hold *taik-pan,* the flowers of the Honolulu creeper, for the drawing-room, but she always preferred a religious use for such noble and valuable objects. I liked all these bowls very much; they had good proportions, round the rim and base was a border of formal scroll design and, within this chaste frame, the elephants, princes, trees and *nat* spirits waved and bounded in profusion. At the base of each bowl was a felicitous salutation inscribed on a smooth ground.

Lacquer is another industry now turning out cigar and trinket boxes, table mats, bowls and other articles for the modern market, but also continuing to supply all Burmese households with objects for daily use. When my father was stationed at Magwe, we went up the river to Pagan and from there by bullock cart to the village of Nyaung-U, where the best Burmese lacquer is made. A frame of bamboo strips woven closely is covered and filled out with a mixture of cow-dung and paddy husk, and given a thick coat of black *thitsi,* wood-oil. Traditional designs are engraved on this when dry, and successive coatings of thitsi mixed with coloring are put on, the bowl being allowed to dry and turned on a lathe to take off the color not required in the pattern in between each coating. The finished product is polished smooth and so flexible that a bowl can be bent till the opposite sides of its rim touch. We had lacquer boxes, *yun-its,* of great size to hold my father's turbans and my mother's scarves, round ones to hold combs and tresses for my mother's hairdressing, drinking mugs, betel boxes and many others. We had *kyauk-ka,* a more solid lacquer of plain red and black, for food carriers with plates and cups to match.

Wood seems part of the fabric of the Burmese craftsman's being. The wealth of the forests which provided teak, pyinkado, ingyin and a host of other woods for lasting structures; the perfect medium they afforded to the chisel, gouge and mallet of the carver, and the traditional forms of architecture, which offered vantage points for the display of superb craftsmanship, all combined to make wood-carving the most lively of Burmese arts. But wood-carving cannot be seen to advantage in domestic articles; we had carved wooden frames for photographs of monks and of Grandfather, carving on the screen which walled off the altar room, but Burmese carvers in wood had never devoted their talents to the cutting of small articles. Teak and *yamanè*, the two woods usually carved on, have a coarse grain in which fine detail cannot be rendered. Beginning from the days when the tradition was to reserve carving for the wood of sacred structures only—palaces and monasteries—the craftsman had put all his skill into animating the gables and eaves of tiered monastery roofs, palace walls and ceilings, with a riot of living ogres, nats, dancing spirits and birds surrounded by leaves, flowers and scroll work which did not leave an inch bare.

Still, the village craftsman with a talent for work in wood does not lack scope in his rural surroundings.

His constructive skill with wood has been most successfully expressed in the vehicles for land and water transport—the bullock cart and the canoe. The classic pattern for a Burmese boat is the *laung*, built from a single hollowed-out trunk of the *thingan*, a tough tree growing near the water with a girth of four to twenty feet and a height of fifteen to seventy-five feet. The trunk is hollowed out into a rough hull, the outside is adzed, circles of holes are bored through for a guide, and the shell is hollowed to a uniform thickness. It is then waterlogged, and fired slowly, the symmetry being carefully tended as the hull opens out with the firing. Planks are built up on the sides to increase capacity. These laungs, of a capacity from ten to forty tons, are the universal canoes of the rivers and creeks of Burma. Poled upstream and rowed downstream, they are ideal in the ease with which they can be bumped against rocks or got off shoals, the thingan hull lasting for twenty or thirty years. The bigger boats which still carry rice and other produce up the Irrawaddy are built up from stout ribs on a style which simulates the solid hull of the laung. These boats carry enormous sails and a crew of

brass ware

about fifteen men. Their bulkheads are richly carved, and they glide along the great Irrawaddy, stately and calm beside the chugging river-steamers, their prows rising and falling like the heads of some fabulous birds.

The Burmese cart is a poem in curves of wood. The floor of the cart gives a slight curving sweep from front to back, the sides exaggerate this in crescents that sweep right up into the air, and the circle of the wheel has good balance and strength behind its symmetry. For the sake of the curves, the root wood of cutch and the curved branches of thingan are specially sought out.

Brassware, for which the old centres were at Amarapura and Sagaing in Upper Burma, we were familiar with in bells and gongs. Bells are kept by the Burmese for sacred uses only. The delicate small bells hung high around the spires of pagodas, often of gold and silver, have tongues that are moved by the winds to give a sweet testimony, to all spirits, of the good work of men who built the pagoda and other men who pray below, and give the praying devotee a tinkling reassurance of his merit. The great bells, however, made of molten copper and tin poured into moulds of clay and wax in pits dug in the earth, have no tongues;

but when struck with deer's antlers or a wooden striker they sing a deep note of sweetness. The names given to some famous bells reflect their beauty: *Maha Ganda* (Great Voice), *Mahati Thadda Ganda* (Great Sweet Sound). All big bells are hung on a cross bar with wooden supports at pagodas, where after recitation of precepts we picked up the striker in turn and struck three times to announce to the spirits around that we had meritoriously praised the Lord Buddha, and then touched the earth with the striker to pass the message to the spirits there also. These big bells may weigh up to twenty-five tons; the bell at Mingun is said to be the second largest in the world. They are all inscribed with lauds and invocations for the welfare of the donor. Gongs of brass are the bells of the town-crier; all announcements are punctuated with the striking of a gong. *Maung le htu tè* is the equivalent of "broadcasting it around the town." Much attention is paid to the melodiousness of gongs; for the Burmese have a musical instrument called the *kyi-waing*, which is a circular frame on which graduated gongs are hung and beaten with a knobbed stick to harmonize with the rest of a Burmese orchestra.

There were numerous other objects for which my mother would never accept a substitute from English shops because they did not cater for our ingrained customs. Soup never tastes right when eaten with a metal spoon—we always used Burmese china spoons bought for about one anna each; rice is not to be stirred with a metal utensil either—the Burmese wooden ladle for this is the *yaung-ma*, the same word as for sister-in-law, the stirrer of trouble. There were, of course, particular places in Burma which supplied particular articles of dress, but I took an interest in this only when I was grown up.

What delights me is to find now that, in the imported things about the house also, all minkadaw households bought a standard type. This was probably due to the enterprise of Messrs. Rowe and Co., a Rangoon firm selling general goods, which established branches in all district towns to provide officers with anything they could not buy in native shops. We all bought Gold Medal

imported articles

camp chairs and camp cots from Rowe's. We bought durwan's kerosene lamps for bedrooms, Storm King and Petromax lamps with incandescent mantles for sitting and dining rooms, we bought crockery which came out in three or four good standard patterns, with an adaptation from the orthodox English dinner service to provide soup and curry dishes suitable for Burmese meals. We got cane furniture made in the local jails, odd chairs and always the half-wood half-cane stores box to serve on tours, and the long basket trays in which my father's files and papers would come home and go to the office every day, on the head of the *chaprassi*. The *hpas*, soft expandable cane boxes in which Burmese people pack their bedding when travelling, were always covered with green canvas from Rowe's. With these hpas, matching the Gold Medal camp cots and chairs, the boxes from the jails, a clerk and two or three girls looking after the children, and a general air of solicitous attention from the people around, no one could mistake an a-so-ya government official's family on its touring travels.

chapter 3

Childhood games—spirits—stories—medicines—horoscopes —children and parents—family outings—the shinbyu *cere-mony for boys*

WHEN I was about five years old, my young brother, the third child of the family, died suddenly and created a gap of about seven years between me and the next child. My brother and I thus grew up apart from my younger sisters for a good part of our childhood.

Two boys were brought up to play with my brother and help my mother with the garden: I was given Mya Shwe to play with. A-Shwe and I were very attached to each other and liked the same games. Burmese children are not as interested in dolls, balls, animals and other toys as the European child; our treasures were chiefly in the form of seeds, which play the same part in Burmese children's games as balls do in Western games. We had

playing with seeds

go-nyin, round flat seeds about two inches wide, from a jungle creeper which grew in my grandmother's garden in Ye. We rolled these along the ground to hit other go-nyins, like ninepins. When the family ate custard apples we collected all the seeds and washed them. These seeds provided us with several games; we scattered them in front of us and tried to flick as many as possible into a hole dug into the ground, or sometimes to flick each seed to touch another, removing one each time it touched until we could clear all the scattered seeds.

We could do this with tamarind seeds too: these were pretty black shining ones. We could get them from the kitchen but always preferred to take one of the boys on walks to tamarind trees. Hla Aung climbed the tree and brought down a cluster of fruits surrounded by delicate feathery leaves. We took a packet of salt along and ate the acid fruit dipped in salt, against all orders; we shredded the leaves till we got a big pile, wrapped them with the rest of the salt in stout paper, buried it a few inches in the ground and then all took turns at jumping on the spot, shouting: "*Bok-hsi-yay-Hsan, Hsan*: Oh pressed oil, come sprinkle, sprinkle." The moisture from the fresh leaves came out with the stamping and dissolved the salt, making a lovely savory mess of the crushed leaves which we unearthed after a while and ate greedily. Then A-Shwe and I carried home the seeds to add to our collection.

Kha-yay si also we collected. These are seeds of the *kha-yay,* a tall tree which scatters its ripe fruit on the ground, where they lie until they dry, and shed their flesh and leave the seeds hidden among the grass and leaves for us to find. But expeditions to the kha-yay trees were approved of because the tree also scatters pretty white starry flowers of a delicate fragrance; the beautiful ladies in my dreams always wore *kha yay pan* in their hair. A-Kyi took us on these walks; we collected seeds, and the flowers we deposited in cane sieve trays; when we got home we helped her to thread them in garlands, the first for the altar, next for my mother's hair and the rest for A-Kyi and the girls. Our tiniest seeds were the *yway si*, seeds of the *adenanthera* tree, bright red and black seeds about the size of an orange pip. Goldsmiths use them as their lowest unit of weight, ninety-six of these seeds forming one tola. They were very difficult to find and I used to pun and call them *ma-yway si* (cannot pick seeds), but it was exciting to turn over a leaf and see the seed suddenly, like a bright ladybird asleep.

My brother was very scornful about our girlish *sètauk-tè*, seed flicking games, but sometimes when Hla Aung and Hla Maung were working he would join in the *son-la ma-la* game, guessing whether a pile of seeds was *son*, a pair, that is, even; or *ma*, female, that is, odd. We could play this to gamble our privileges or possessions on the strength of guessing right. I always annoyed my brother at this game; when it came to my turn to pose the question I would take as great a pile as my two hands could cover because I loved counting. My father told me I was mathematical, and so I had counted everything I could; I knew the number of steps leading up to every pagoda we had visited, how many matches there were in a box, how many holes the latticework round our house contained, and now I counted hundreds of custard apple seeds while my brother tried his best not to hit me, to swallow his impatience to see whether he had guessed right or wrong. He himself hated to count.

On moonlight nights my mother gave permission for A-Kyi and the other girls to play with us in the company of the male servants and clerks. We played *bi-yaung-tan*, the comb seller, in which we formed a long row one behind the other to form the teeth of a comb, and after a long altercation between the head of the row—the seller—and the catcher, the latter tried to catch the end person on the row. Or we drew lines of white lime on the red gravel road outside and played *htok-si-tan*, in teams, one team "keeping" the lines and the other dashing through until a member got trapped by the keepers. I can still see the long line of the human comb waving sinuously as the players ran to and fro, and the straight white lines of the htok-si-tan, as patterns in

children's games

the flood of moonlight. They were invariably broken by a bout of "cock-fighting" to exhaust everyone's legs and lungs and spirits before bed.

The Burmese representation of a cock walk is to sit on the haunches, and then slide each foot forward and sideways while in that position, in imitation of the webbed feet of a fowl. Done in quick tempo it becomes an acrobatic or a dancer's feat to sitters on chairs, but Burmans do it easily. We broke up into two teams and put out a prize cock in turn. The two cocks face each other and shuffle out their legs slowly to the rhythm of the accompanying verse: a slow and measured beat at first, then a sudden quickening with the acceleration of the rhythm, until at the crow given by the teams both go all out, quicker and quicker until one is exhausted and falls out vanquished. This is what we sang in chorus:

Kyet Hpa ta nyin — Two cocks, a fine pair
Taw go win — Walk in the forest dare
Maung Yin la, lay hnin pyit. — Comes Maung Yin and shoots with bow.

Ma pyit ba hnin, — O Maung Yin, don't shoot so,
Maung Yin yè — Styes will on your eyelids grow.°
Kyet-tet su tat tè. — On the left eye, one two!
Bè beka su su — On the right eye, one two!
Nya beka su su — Come my friend then let us fight it!
Khut laik gya so thu-ngè-gyin!

Aw-ee-ee-uu! — Cock-a-doodle doo!
Nga do kyet hpa naing naing — Our cock will win it, win it!
Thu do kyet hpa shon shon. — Their cock will finish, finish!

Some of the games included forfeits, but the forfeits were of a broad comicality, dragging the victim by the ear, or if it happened to be one of the younger servants, rubbing soot on his

---

° There is a belief that styes are retribution for the killing of a cock.

face. Robbing stones from under the care of a guardian keeping
watch over them within a circle was stealing the eggs from a
mother tortoise; the postless figure in General Post was a *khway-
yu*, mad dog; blind man's buff was *bok-ta-lon tauktè*, a tucktoo
with a buff.

We spent a lot of time with A-Kyi and the men about the
house. It was they who filled our world with bogies and spirits
who were no less real to them than they were to us. We were
warned not to be too greedy, or we would turn into *peik-tas* in
the next existence, great tall spirits with voracious appetites and
mouths the size of a needle's eye, or others with mouths like
yawning caverns wide enough to swallow a pig, but no stomachs
to receive the food. We were told that miserly and avaricious
people would never be parted from their possessions, which
would follow them into their next existence, when they would be
ok-ta-sauk, pictured for us as assuming the guise of fair girls
with thanakha on their faces and flowing hair, fair until they had
enticed young men into the treasure dens, when they would suddenly turn into old women. There were also *ta-says* who haunted
human beings, *son-ma* witches who disguised themselves until
they were ready to eat you, and *belus*, ogres which thrived on
human beings. Far from the careful nurturing which is given to
modern children of the West in attempts to prevent fears of the
dark and loneliness, in Thanatpin I could have pointed out the
actual tree in which the old witch lived, and when it grew dark
both my nurse and I would shiver together in each other's arms
at the thought of it.

Nor were the funny stories of the right type for Western children, though they made us roar with delight. There were two
brothers who wanted to make their grandmother beautiful, and
bathed her in the hottest water they could produce; the water
was boiling and the grandmother emerged clean and fair and
rigid, and the two grandsons dressed her up and propped her in
the doorway for all to admire. There was also the monkey who

from his perch in a tree above the bazaar shouted: "Whoever eats of the fruit of this tree will have fragrant gases in his body." One poor human fool believed him, and ate, and went around hawking his ware of fragrant gases. He came to the court of the king, who caused seven layers of curtains to shroud the chamber for fear any of the fragrance would be lost when the experiment was carried out. We laughed to tears at the account of the poor fool's discomfiture.

When we were to be given any medicines or had any pain, however, both my father and mother waited on us. We did not use Western medicines in the house. We always had stocks of various kinds of *yet-sa*, a linctus powder with digestive qualities containing licorice and herbs in a salt base. The taste is pleasant to all Burmese people, who eat it at the slightest provocation; excess of it causes no harm. There is a popular brand on the market called *lay-myo shit-sè*, eighty kinds of wind, but in addition to this, each family gets a specially prepared type from their family monk. My father, who was interested in herbal medicine, collected recipes and my mother compounded them at home. We ate yet-sa whenever we had a slight stomach ache or when my mother considered that the food had been too rich. For a general tonic my father got from the monk a honey mixture with special powers, partly owing to the holiness of the monk, and we ate a tiny spoonful of this each night after prayers. For coughs and sore throats we had pills, called *hpongyi-bo-sha-na,* from Moulmein. They were made of pepper, capsicum, licorice and salt, and acted by stimulating the salivary and throat juices.

All these medicines had a pleasant taste and we liked eating them, but when we had a fever we were given *ngan-say*, a black powder of herbs and salt, which was mixed with hot water and given to us in saucers, my mother invoking the Triple Gems while blowing on it and coaxing us to drink it as the medicine of the Three Gems: "*Paya-say, taya-say, thanga-say*," she would say: "Physic of the Buddha, of the Law, of the Clergy." After this came two saucersful of hot water in which betel leaves had been boiled, to raise a sweat; my mother would cover us with an ok-saung, my father would come in on tiptoe to look at us very often, even when our temperatures were nearly normal, and the fever would leave us quite soon.

Our purgative was *dat-le-ba-say*, physic of the four elements; it was a glutinous paste of senna for purging, tamarind as acid and purgative, jaggery to sooth, licorice to taste, and salt. It was nasty. My mother rolled about a golf ball size of the stuff into little balls which we were expected to swallow. But she was very firm that there must always be an odd number of balls, because Burmese people believe that odd numbers are more auspicious, like the *Three* Gems, the *Nine* Nawaya; when the shinbyu cere-mony for the initiation of boys into the priesthood is carried out, or the ears of the girls bored ceremonially, it is inauspicious to "do" an even number of children. So if my mother's golf ball of the purgative made eight balls, she would always pinch more stuff out of the jar and make nine, and, as I grew older and more skeptical, both my stomach and my mood would react on each other and I generally got stuck at the sixth or eighth, much to my mother's dismay. But to this day I believe in the efficacy of these particular medicines for my own system.

When any of us kept ailing over a long period it was felt that our astronomical prospects were low, and the *bedin-saya*, vul-garly translated as fortune-teller, was called in. He was regarded as an astrologer. My mother brought out our horoscopes, which had been cast by a Brahmin when we were a few years old. These horoscopes, inscribed on a palm leaf doubled up and sewn tightly together, were precious objects kept at the head of my father's bed. The exact day and hour of the birth of the child, the auspicious name given according to this time and day, the astronomical bodies exerting influence over such a birth, and a table to show the heavenly influences which would prevail dur-ing the successive periods of the child's life so that future calculations could be made, were all inscribed finely on this neat yellow leaf. The bedin-saya made calculations now to see if our *kan* (fate, luck) was high or low; if low, he prescribed some counteracting influences.

I was once given a chicken as a *khamè*, a charm which would keep the evil influences at bay, and the servants fed the chicken for me until I had recovered. Sometimes it is certain foods which bring the evil influences, and the proscribing of them even during good health was more annoying. One of my sisters, treated thus as a child, complained that the bedin-saya was a tiresome old man with rhetorical leanings and included things because they formed a nice rhyme, and, indeed, she was not far from the truth. Our monosyllabic language is a heavenly gift to us with its endless scope for the most unrestrained punning and rhyming; the pun in Burmese is not execrable humor but a stepping-stone for flights of fancy. What my sister was not allowed to eat were the three most precious foods as proverbialized in: *a-thi-hma tha-yet; a-ywet hma la-hpet; a-tha hma wet:* among fruits the *tha-yet,* among leaves the *la-hpet,* among flesh the *wet: tha-yet, la-hpet* and *wet* being the mango, the pickled tea-leaf and the pig's flesh respectively, and open to question as being really the prize specimens of their class, but certainly rhyming happily.

My parents were so good to us; they never scolded, beat or punished us that I can remember. Perhaps they had both had so much discipline in their own youths; I can remember the day we were told to answer them "Father" and "Mother" when they called us, instead of *Paya* as we had done formerly. Paya is the term of extreme respect and humility, sometimes adopted by children to parents, always by servants to their superiors, by subordinates to senior officials, and by all to royalty and the clergy. It is also the suffix to honorific titles. Its true and ancient use had associations of reverence only, but it has taken on a more subservient hue with the advent of government and foreign officials.

But whether we answered Paya or Father, my mother's guiding influence led us to look on my father with awe, even though he was the parent who clowned with us at home. We were always bathed and dressed before he came home, waiting for him. As soon as he entered the gate we raced down the drive to carry his umbrella, took him upstairs and scrambled to take his shoes off as soon as we could get him seated. His shoes, suspenders and socks were removed by combined efforts, my father pretending great helplessness all the while. We went for walks while my parents went to play tennis, but returned in time to carry their rackets upstairs and remove my father's shoes again. After dinner my mother and we lay on mats while my father sat in an easy chair and pretended to get his nursery rhymes all wrong, until we taught him:

A-hpo gyi oh, hka kon kon,	Old man so bent and gray,
Ma thay ba hnin ohn	Do not die as yet we pray.
Naung hnit-kha ta-saung-mon	Till next December try to tarry
Pwè kyi ba ohn.	And watch the actors play and marry.

Or the voracious cat who ate everything:

Kyaung-gyi yè tè mi tan to	Oh you big and short tailed cat.
A-hsi ko sa ba lo	Swallowing the lean
A-tha ko myo.	And eating the fat.

Or of far-off Meiktila Lake, where the water stretches seven miles long:

Meiktila kan-daw auk ka	From the waters of Meiktila Lake
Hpa kauk hkè ba	Pick up a frog for me.
Hpa pa yin ta gaung pay ba	Poor little frog,
Myet lon ga kyaung taung taung hnin,	Eyes big agog,
Hpa gaung ga thay.	And body so thin and wee.

Or the jumping nonsensical rhyme about Gyat-Aye, who got beaten by her mother and wept in a dark corner and started a train of kaleidoscopic events, for every time a line ended with a clanging rhythm it suggested a rhyming word to shout out and continue its own associations, and when you got back to a rhyme for Gyat-Aye, you had to start all over again, and poor Gyat-Aye got beaten and cried as long as children's voices held out.

Gyat-Aye	Gyat-Aye
Thu amay yaik lo	Beat by her mother so,
Hmaung maik hma ngo	Cries in dark corner "O,"
Ko Lu Byo	Young bachelor Ko
Hta-yan pauk ka	Through hole in the mantel
Chay-dauk ko-swè	Pulls at her ankle
Twè-lè!	Dangle!
Twè-le yè	Dangling yet wait awhile,
Nay ba ohn	The rain clouds pile,
Mo tway ka chon	The heavens clang.
Mok lon!	Meringue!
Mok lon yè sekku kat pa lo	Meringue with paper stuck below
Kya-ka-lat hnin hsun-daw tin	Offer at altar in lacquer bowl,
Pa-lin paw ka myauk kalay,	From throne seat the monkey gay
Hsin chi lo pyay	Runs down and off with it away!
Gyat-Aye!	Gyat-Aye!

Before going to bed, A-Kyi or Ngwe Yin took us in to say our prayers in chorus. We then *shikkoed* our parents, that is, made obeisance to them by folding hands and bowing till our foreheads and outstretched palms touched the ground, first to my father, then to my mother, and they said in turn each night: "*Pongyi-ba-say, thetshay-ba-say meba hnin-o-aung-min-aung paung-ya-ba-say:* May your holiness be great and your life long, may you be united with your parents even until the attainment of old age."

The social life which my parents led with other families in the district towns was shared by us and all the other children. Bur-

mese children do not live in a child's world cut off from reality—
there is no specially created world for them like that of J. M.
Barrie—they are given enough food for their wildest imagination, but this feeds equally the grandmother and nurses who tell
them stories. No special children's parties with cakes and games
for them are provided; they go everywhere with the grown-ups,
on visits, excursions and festivals, they eat and sleep in the same
rooms as the elders and hear most of the conversation. One result is to make Burmese children more conscious of family ties
and responsibilities, and to prepare them better for any calamities
that may befall them in adolescence or any time before they are
fully grown up. Yet no one who sees Burmese children can doubt
that delight, wonder and pure joy are present in their lives.

All Burmese social gatherings center round either religious
observances or eating. We are still unsophisticated enough to
have the same way of enjoying ourselves whether in city or country, and for that reason these district towns formed such a perfect
background for happy days. In the towns that I remember, a
river ran through, with sandbanks at edges or in midstream; this,
with the monasteries and pagoda precincts a little way out of the
busy quarters, private garden orchards and the houses of friends,
provided the background for all the social life which my parents
had, and is the reason why Burmese people never form social
clubs. Most of the officials went to play tennis at the Gymkhana
club with European members, but it had no real part in their
lives.

When we went on *pyaw-pwè-sas,* happy-eating-gatherings, at
pagodas, with two or three other families, the grown-ups, including aunts and dependents of the families, made elaborate food
arrangements because the joy of the occasion was to cook on a
large scale in the open air. They took pots, dishes, food,
washing apparatus for about twenty people. We started with
silent recitation of prayers before the golden spire in the cool
morning air, holding silver lilies between folded hands and being
so careful not to breathe in the fragrance of the flowers, because

picnics at the pagoda

my mother taught us that we should not first enjoy the beauty of flowers which are to be offered. When our short prayers were through, we stuck the flowers in a vase or niche at the pagoda base, lighted a row of candles along a ledge or parapet, and walked quietly round the pagoda with the paved stones so cool beneath our bare feet, while the grown-ups still prayed silently. As soon as they finished and got up, it was the signal to release our spirits and bound away to the far corner, where the servants were already beginning to unpack the pots and arrange three stones around for each fire. We were allowed to cut up onions or chillies until we got bored, and spent the rest of the morning playing games or exploring the country around, coming back to find a meal miraculously cooked, with curries in lacquer dishes and rice in banana leaves. After the meal, mats were spread in the breeziest spot, and we lay down beside the grown-ups, who told beads and talked by turns.

Garden orchards were another source of deep long whole-day joy. The Burmese *u-yin* is usually translated as orchard, but after seeing English apple and cherry orchards I must translate it more fully. An u-yin is more arboreal and leafy; also one must enjoy it positively, that is, there must be in it a bamboo or light wooden house. In a hot climate an u-yin raises visions of shade; cool dark shade, leaves, only a few flowers unless they are of flowering trees, eating of the fruits and vegetables while there, and lying on a mat in the afternoon breeze. None of the a-so-ya mins could possess u-yins or gardens like this where they were posted, because their stay was so transitory. But the education officer, that is, the D.I.S. (District Inspector of Schools), whether active or retired, was usually more permanent and could dig his toes in more happily. The social relationship was also ideal. Earning less than the other officials, he could yet offer them this rich hospitality of natural pleasures.

When we were in Maubin the D.I.S. was our friend U Taik Wan. He and his family of ten sons and daughters had the u-yin developed to its fullest. He had a low large house where the rivei took a bend and had fenced in this bed with bamboo stakes and a diving platform. The garden orchard stretched away from the house to a bamboo hut at the far end, with open verandahs under the trees. The specialty of his orchard were his sweet-sour marian trees. The marian is the *bonea Burmanica*, common to Burma and northern Assam, where it forms an ideal appetizer for the heat-drowsy inhabitants. It is sour, of a sharp biting sourness which now makes my mouth water with longing. It is too sour to eat except doused in strong salt sauce or fish paste, salt being our antidate to sourness, in which I differ from the English idea of cooking, for salt combines and merges in with sourness whereas a pound of sugar thrown into a gooseberry tart would still leave it too sour for me. The marian is a small fruit, green when young and orange-yellow when ripe, with a pretty purple seed which has given its name to the Burmese color "mauve." There is a sweet variety which is not popular. Sometimes, however, a prize tree is found which produces a sweet-sour marian, a sour fruit with its sting taken off. Such a tree should be treated with the greatest care; its fruits must never be salted or pickled as sour fruits are treated, because the "sour" use would communicate itself to the tree by what may be called sympathetic magic. Rather, my mother made jam (with sugar) of these marians, for the improvement of U Taik Wan's tree.

My mother was very punctilious about such things; the girl servants were never allowed to pluck the citron leaves for our salad because a woman in menstruation makes the tender leaves of the citron tree curl up and lose their succulence when she plucks them. U Taik Wan had a row of sweet-sour marian trees which he guarded from flying foxes by throwing a net across one face of them, showing a wall of these creatures hanging head downwards, to passers-by.

Our pyaw-pawè-sas at the Taik Wans' always began with a lot of water-fun. We never used bathing dresses, but adapted our longyis for swimming. This longyi is shaped and wrapped, like the more famous sarong, at the waist normally, but women and girls take it above the bosom when they discard their jackets. This enables all our poorer women to bathe with perfect decorum at public wells and streams. After the bath a dry longyi is slipped on over the wet one which is then washed clean straightaway. The poorest, who do not always possess a spare longyi, sometimes let themselves into a stream gradually, lifting the longyi higher as they go in, and when the water is bosom-high they keep the garment on their head, letting it down again as they emerge. Our use for the adaptability of the longyi was to stand on a diving platform with it open wide at the bottom, jump feet first and let the air rush in, nicking the longyi in at the ankles as we struck the water. This makes you land with a balloon which floats you for a minute or two like those swollen celluloid ducks in babies' tubs. My friend Tin Tin Thoung was just like a swan on these occasions; she was not pretty normally, being very thin and angular, but she had a long and graceful neck, and when she floated on the water, gliding along with her neck rising out of her big round longyi, she looked like a beautiful swan to me. After bathing, the Taik Wans' mother had basketfuls of Indian corn, the tender ones boiled and the tougher ones roasted, and dishes of the peeled marians doused in fish sauce awaiting us.

Besides these social visits there were special festivals that came with the months, and occasions common to every family's history—the ear-boring of the girl, the initiation into the priesthood of the boy, and marriages of grown-up children—which had to be celebrated in traditional forms. Most minkadaws preferred to hold marriage ceremonies in Rangoon, Moulmein or Mandalay to have as much fashion and show as possible, but the ear-boring (*nadwin*) and initiation into priesthood (*shinbyu*) find a better background in country towns. Nadwin is the coming of age of a girl, not for marriage, but for the initiation into the pleasant vanities of a woman's life. It is fine enough to sit with a rich and full dress on a cushion, the center of the crowd of people who have been invited for feasting, to have the ears pierced with a gold pin and after this always to wear diamond ear-rings, but the ceremony has no deeper significance than that the parent feels he has done the best for his daughter at this stage of her life. The shinbyu, however, is much more than a social event. It has a religious meaning of the fullest beauty.

Although the women of Burma figure as actively and have the same rights as men in the fields of business, property and professions of the modern world, we always keep alive in us the religious feeling that we are "below" mankind. It is not so much a feeling that women are a lower race as that a man has the nobility of manhood in him. We call it *hpon,* the glory, the holiness of a man, and we respect this not with subservience but with the same feelings as we respect monks and parents. A wife does not throw her longyi across her husband's bed, she does not touch any of his possessions with her feet in carelessness, she uses a separate mug for her bathwater. A bad wife who does not respect her husband's manhood does him the greatest harm, for a man cannot prosper if his hpon is hampered; indeed, some women who indulge in black magic deliberately *hpon-nein* their husbands, that is, lower his hpon by carelessly wielding brooms above his head, throwing women's longyis on his pillow, thus making him subordinate, and believing that this makes the wife's will prevail over the husband's. But such a man can never make progress in his career.

It is the Buddhist belief that the attainment of a perfect life is as a man, as shown in Gautama Buddha's life as Prince Siddhartha. Prince Siddhartha was the son of King Suddhodana, who surrounded his son with all the luxury and splendor that his kingdom on the slopes of the Himalayas could offer. To prevent his son from renouncing his princely life for one of poverty and meditation he kept all sight of sorrow, sickness and decay hidden from him. He found him a perfect wife, beautiful, meek and affectionate, who bore him a son; but the prince in his excursions to a park in the city came across a decrepit old man, a sick old man and a corpse, which sights made him sad at the thought of human misery in this world. The next time, however, he saw a hermit, which suggested that peace of mind was achievable by renunciation of the vanities of the world. On the night that his son was born, Prince Siddhartha made the Great Renunciation and left everything to go into solitude and find out the cause of misery, and the means of its removal. The Dhammapada says of the world:

> Come! behold this world which is like a decked royal chariot, wherein the foolish immerse themselves; but for the wise there is no attachment.

It is this renunciation which we symbolize in the shinbyu ceremony when a boy leaves his home and lives in the order. A parent who fails to hold the ceremony or get his son initiated in some other way fails in his first duty towards his son, and those who hold a shinbyu for orphans or the son of the poor achieve great merit.

To provide a background symbolic of Prince Siddhartha's circumstances, parents spend as much as they can afford; a flagged pavilion is put up before the house, a multitude of people are invited for feasting, the boy is dressed in princely garments and jewels, and rides around the town on a white horse, with a procession following. For him to return and wash the powder off his face, to doff the turban and show the newly shaven head, to change the glittering clothes of silk for a plain yellow robe showing golden on the bare brown skin,—this is moving indeed. And when he comes back the next day in procession with other monks, his eyes cast down and his bowl before him, his mother makes obeisance to him for the first time, not as her son now but as one of the priestly order, a hpongyi, a "great glory." That must be a moment of spiritual plenitude in a mother's life.

I do not remember much about my brother's shinbyu, but I remember the beauty of his face as he came back in procession on that first day. A good face has its nobility enhanced by the complete absence of such adornment, even as is provided by the frame of hair or the line of neck clothing; it has to stand alone. I am often struck with the beautiful calm faces of some older monks. There is a look of repose which they wear easily after years of daily meditation and freedom from petty irritations and personal relationships, and a glow to the brown skin which is the result of years spent in clean and open surroundings, with sufficient to eat, and regularity of hours; the strongly marked eyebrows giving a nobility to the face when the head has been shorn. The unconscious reflection of this look on the face of a small boy touches us profoundly; there is a sweet solemnity on the young shaven face; the most mischievous boys become awed and chastened without any prompting.

In recent years, we have had a full dress shinbyu in the family for my husband's nephew, Sao Sai Long, who as the heir to the Shan State of Kengtung was initiated into the priesthood with the full panoply due to Buddhist royalty. A long wide bamboo pavilion was set up, beginning with a high shelf for the offerings to all the monasteries in the town, the next platform for the monks who were to receive Sao Sai Long into their monastery, the next lower for the attendant boys who were also to be initiated, and for the *palin* (the jewelled *chaise longue* on which Sao Sai Long was to recline), the next for the family, and successively lower ones for the various grades of the people. (The European officials and friends were given chairs in deference to their stiffer joints, but the chairs which eventually raised them higher than the family were placed on a side platform which had been cleverly made two inches lower than the family's platform.) On the day of the actual initiation, tall vases on the high shelf held robes, fans and slippers as offerings to the monks, and rupee coins put into long net cylinders to get around the rule that monks should not touch money. Sitting against this were a row of monks with eyes downcast, below and before them were the *shinlaungs,* sixteen little attendant boys all powdered white with silk clothes and golden chains around their necks. On the couch sat Sao Sai Long, Sao Thiri Raza, his face unpowdered but glowing with the beauty of his race, his clothes of finest silk and gold, on his head a jewelled crown sitting proudly above his young face.

Three days in succession before the actual initiation day he sat like this in front of the assembled people, and when the drums took up the strange sad music which is traditionally played for the departure of a king, he stepped into a throne-seat that was lifted high on an elephant to go in procession round the town. The music and the splendor of Buddhist kingship in these days of government officials stirred the unrealized, half-forgotten roots in our breasts, it made us feel things we had known in some other world and brought tears to our eyes. Sao Sai Long, my nephew aged fourteen, who had just returned from a year at King's School, Canterbury, who had never given me a moment's peace with his affectionate and irreverent ways, and who is even now riding wildly round an Australian sheep farm, felt and looked a dignity which he has never achieved before or since, as he was lifted high on an elephant and rode around his beautiful old city with its big trees and mountains, with spears, banners, white and gold umbrellas before him, a king for the last time in full pomp. He must have felt like Tamurlaine:

> Oh, 'tis passing fair to be a king,
> And ride in triumph through Persepolis.

chapter 4

My father's birthday—monastic and secular education—the autumn festival—government administration—women's jewellery—helping relatives

Round about the end of January each year, for our lunar dates do not fall on the same calendar dates every year, we celebrated my father's birthday. All Burmese celebrations have a basis of "doing merit" either in feasting people and perhaps fasting oneself, distributing gifts, or inviting monks to preach and others to hear them. An atmosphere of enjoyment is possible in these good works because Burmese people do not believe in divorcing their praying from their merry-making: usually both are carried out in the same room, the pleasure after the holiness; and the donor feels a great satisfaction of spirit as he says: "*A-hmya a-hmya:* Share with all (the merit from his good deed)." The friends gathered around reply to this "*Tha-du, tha-du:* Well done, well done."

On my father's birthday monks were "lifted" or invited to the house for a grand meal. All the Western chairs and tables were moved out of the sitting room; and one end of the room was laid with carpets of red and green rose design, specially kept for such occasions in all Burmese houses. This was for the monks to sit on and facing them the people would sit on mats. Between the monks and people were laid out all the presents for the monastery.

I was always sad when I saw these presents; to my childish eyes they looked so uninteresting. A monk who renounces worldly goods is allowed to possess only eight articles, three pieces of cloth which form his robes, a begging bowl, a mat, a blade, a needle and a water strainer. Dagas or donators can, therefore, only give these, or other articles necessary to the way of life conforming to their precepts. This can include religious books, mats, candles and matches, brooms, spittoons. These last make very elegant presents, and are a common sight at all distributions of presents, the standard pattern being of white enamel, with a red band around the edge. Children are told of one monastery whose holiness is so high that a spittoon donated to the monks there will echo the name of the donator each time a monk spits into it. With the presents all laid out, the monks walked in a row, and sat with eyes downcast and legs crossed. My mother and father made obeisance to them and sent for us after a few words with the chief monk. We were always nervous and subdued on these occasions; in speaking to a monk a vocabulary of honorifics has to be used, even for "yes." The hpongyi always made joking inquiries about whether we were getting enough Buddhist and Burmese teaching for we were attending English Christian schools at the time.

The monks have lost all touch with the schooling of the great majority of children by now. In the first decade of the century the monastic schools were still the backbone of instruction for boys throughout all the rural districts, being responsible for the high literacy figure of 49 per cent for Burman males, as compared with 11.9 per cent in Madras at the time. But lay schools, either established and run on Burman lines, or established by Christian missionary societies with perhaps grants-in-aid, or under the direct management of Government or a committee acting on behalf of the government, were springing up on all sides, until by 1934 the proportion of lay to recognized monastic schools for vernacular education was about five to one. Although there had been attempts to raise the utilitarian value of monastic education by the encouragement of such subjects as arithmetic, geography and land surveying, it was far easier for the lay schools to conform to the standards set by the Board of Examiners. With the passing of such standards becoming the means of obtaining employment and the changing of fashions, more and more children went to the lay schools. Moreover, the lay schools included schools for girls, either separately or in common with boys.

In my childhood there were still echoes of the opposition between monastic and secular education. In about 1922 my Uncle Pyant, who was then a serious student at the University, told me the world was round, "but," he added, "the hpongyis say that this is not true and most elder people don't believe it." My husband also tells me that when he went home from his government school with the statement that the earth spun around on its axis and took twenty-four hours to do it, the elders were most scornful. "In that case," they said, "if you were to go up into the air and stay there for some time, you could not come down to Kengtung until the same time the next day, but might land in England for your lunch."

Another difference between old and new ideas of education was that the elder people were aghast at the long years which a modern education from primary schools to University lasted. They felt that at least one must have learned everything there was to learn by then, for a few years at a monastery taught a boy all the reading, writing, calculation and literature which any grown man was expected to know. Once my grandfather received a telegram announcing the birth of a grandson; the message contained the additional information that the doctors had found it necessary to perform a circumcision on the infant. The telegram was in English, according to the rules of the Posts and Telegraphs in Burma, and Grandfather called my cousin Ko Lu Pe to read it. My cousin had been at a government school for some years and though he could read and write English with some ease, he stuck at the word "circumcise." "What!" exploded Grandfather, "five years learning English, and you can't even read a telegram. This education is quite useless." Whereupon he took the grandchildren and his two young sons out of their schools until his wrath subsided and they quietly started attendance again. It is a popular stage joke also, the B.A. who returns to his village and is asked in good faith by the hpongyi to mend a villager's watch that has gone wrong. The graduate confesses that he cannot mend it. The monk is horrified: "What, passed B.A. and cannot mend a watch?"

So now on my father's birthday the monks ask jokingly and kindly about our school subjects. Their meal is laid out on a low round table, and consists of all the good things my mother can think of, for they have only one main meal in the day. Rice and meat and vegetable dishes are followed by fruit, sweet milky coffee, sweet English cakes. The monastery boys are given their meal outside; the monks, after eating, rise and go, and the boys follow them bearing away the gifts for the monastery. At once there is a general shuffling into more relaxed positions, conversation swells out, we start to scamper around and help to wheel in more round tabes. Then everybody eats, and my father feels a deep sense of well-being.

Our lunar calendar has twelve months in its year, beginning the new year about the middle of April with the month of *Tagu*. Each month contains the twenty-nine to thirty days of the moon's cycle, but the dates are numbered with only fifteen numbers—fifteen waxing days starting from the crescent of the new moon: *la-hsan ta-yet, la-hsan hna-yet*, new moon first day, second day and so on, until the fifteenth and full moon day, *la-pyit nay:* after which come the waning days, *la-hsot*. With this system, we are twelve or thirteen days short of the 365 each year, and hence every second year there occurs a double month of *Waso*, in July and August, which month also starts our Lent. Lent lasts the three months of the monsoon, until *Thadingyut*, in October, when we see it out with light, feasting and much merriment. For the observance of festivals such as New Year and Thadingyut we usually visited relatives, but certain other observances came round each year to us in our own home.

Such is *htamanè-hto*, the making of a comestible known as *htamanè* in vast quantities, for distribution on the first full moon after the harvest. On the full moon night of *Tabodwè* in January-February, the villagers sit up all night in big parties of men and women singing and joking as they make all preparations for the cooking that is to take place at dawn. The basis of htamanè is a glutinous rice called *kaukhnyin*, always associated with fresh country mornings, dew on the grass and smoke from the wood fire, men and women with cheroots and red striped blankets flung over them grouped around the fire. A favorite way of eating kaukhnyin is to put it with a little salt into a bamboo stick that has been cut with a notch to form a bottom, stop the top with a cork of paper and then roast it over a fire. By the time the stick is about to scorch, the rice is cooked and stuck together in a long tube held by a thin white skin from the inside of the bamboo. Cracked open and eaten with fried chicken it is delicious clean food; the best "kaukhnyin legs" and fried chicken were produced at Letpadan, in Tharawaddy district, for many years running. Other kaukhnyin eaters steam it with beans, pile it on lacquer trays and walk around to sell it in the early mornings about six o'clock, serving it on banana leaves, with sesamum salt and shredded coconut sprayed on top.

But htamanè is made ceremonially only once a year. Work parties of women used to come to our house the day before and sit under the trees cutting coconut and ginger into thin slices, shelling peanuts, picking husks out of the kaukhnyin, and win-

the civil service

nowing this and the sesamum in cane trays. At about four the next morning my mother and the rest of the household got up, and helped by one or two of the young men from other houses, they made fires under the trees, put the kaukhnyin in big pans, with oil and all the prepared ingredients, and cooked it for hours, taking turns to stir the sticky mixture all the time while the others sat around the fire smoking and talking. In the early morning we put the htamanè into dishes for the monasteries and all the houses in the neighborhood, into tins for sending away to relatives in other towns, and store-jars for keeping in the house to eat between meals.

These accounts of our life in the districts are of ceremonies and celebrations so far because I was a child in those days. My parents had their own pattern of life with a background of work. My father, as I have said, belonged to the Burma Civil Service, Class II. The administrative services in Burma included three grades of Civil Services: the I.C.S., which became the Burma Civil Service I after separation from India, the B.C.S., which then became B.C.S. II, and the Subordinate Civil Service. These three services supplied the executive administrative officers, who were placed in charge of the various-sized units of administration, helped in their government by judicial administrative officers of corresponding ranks, and by officers for police, forests, education, excise and other public services for which a separate recruitment was made.

The myookship which my father obtained in 1912 was the most junior of these posts, usually filled by members of the Subordinate Civil Service and beginners in the B.C.S. II. It entailed the charge of a unit of administration known as the township, a collection of village tracts, with headquarters at a town of about two to five thousand inhabitants. The township officer supervised the administration of villages and the land system, helped in the suppression of crime and revenue collection, acted as government registrar, and carried out duties assigned to him by his senior officer. This was the Subdivisional officer, in charge of two or three townships. Two or three subdivisions were in turn grouped into a district under a Deputy Commissioner, a post attainable by members of the B.C.S. II before their turn of service if they showed talent, but more often held by members of the B.C.S. I. Three to eight districts were grouped in divisions under a Divisional Commissioner who had civil and revenue powers and was responsible to the Governor for every department of public service except special branches directly under the control of the central government. There were eight Divisions in Burma.

When my father was an S.D.O. he had various magisterial, civil and revenue powers. Besides exercising these duties in the Subdivisional headquarters, he toured around the subdivision for about ten days in the month and we sometimes accompanied him. When he was stationed at Myanaung we went to Ingabu, where my mother had good friends, Pauktaing, where there was a great and revered image of Buddha, Kyangin, which had a thriving silk-weaving industry. In a township headquarters like Kyangin we met only the Township Officer although the town was divided into blocks or wards, each of which was under a headman whom my father also had to meet.

But in a village like Pauktaing we came directly into contact with the headman, the *thugyi* or "elder person," who, as a source of local authority over villagers, is a carry-over of the administrative system under the Burmese kings. The headmen in those days were properly described by their name of thugyi. They were chosen by the villagers and assisted in their duties by a group of elders. The headman distributed the burden of the revenue that was due from the village among the villagers and collected it, being allowed a percentage of the collections. He was the village magistrate and sometimes the village judge. New settlers in the village had to obtain his permission to take up abode. The office tended to become hereditary, and in those times when there was little contact between the central government and the local administration of the peasantry, the authority of a good headman was a strong influence that extended over more than one village.

In present times, however, each village has been established as a separate administrative unit under one headman; the Township Officer and the Subdivisional Officer have appeared as higher sources of authority which are present not far away, and the village headman has lost much of his standing as elder person responsible for law and order, retaining chiefly his position as tax-collector. This is to the loss of village administration.

As a-so-ya mins, men like my father had more power and prestige than they had money. The salary of a B.C.S. II Officer, which ranged from Rs. 300/- to Rs. 900/-, was enough to ensure easy living and a certain amount of saving for old age, but instead of the expensive carpets, glass, silver, uniformed servants and tinned foods which we saw in English officials' houses, they had to spend what might seem to foreigners a disproportionate amount on two items: jewellery for the women and financial help to relatives. Jewellery is not a vanity for a Burmese woman but an article of dress, worn both day and night, in varying degrees according to whether she is working or out on pleasure. The word for jewellery does not include any description of gems, but is *let-wut let-sa:* wear for the arms and such. When servant girls enter a household the humblest of them is given a gold chain to hang around her neck or a bangle for her wrist. Thus among the classes who have any money to spare beyond that for mere sustenance, from the more affluent cultivators, the small traders and shopkeepers and clerks, to "rich" landowners, millowners and government officials, a great amount of money is spent on jewellery. Not to have any would be an unbearable shame.

A complete set of jewellery for a well-dressed woman comprises the following articles, all worn together when attending shinbyus, ear-boring and marriage ceremonies, official functions and numerous other occasions. For the hair a *sado,* a hairpin with a single large diamond on the end; a comb with teeth of gold and a row of diamonds set closely along the back of the rim; a *sein-pan gaing,* a gold hairpin with a cluster of flowers to hang and dangle, set with diamonds. These articles have the gold parts embedded in the knot of hair and only show the diamonds. Round the neck are worn the *lè-gat,* a narrow gold collar set widely with diamonds, fitting like a vice; below this a double row of small pearls tied tightly behind with red tassels; the *lè-ton* "trembling necklace"—a "choker" necklace—sitting so that little chains set with diamonds hang from it all around the neck and tremble; a chain with a diamond locket below this. In the ears are worn single diamond studs. On the jacket five diamond buttons, attached to gold rings set with diamonds, fasten the button loops. On the wrists and hands diamond bracelets and as many rings as one has, of rubies, emeralds and sapphires set with diamonds, are worn. A young girl also wears hollow anklets of gold round her ankles. In addition to the above, the richer minka-daws and wives of big traders possess corresponding pieces of rubies, emeralds and sapphires to wear in the house or on informal occasions. No wonder a man groans when his wife bears him four daughters to be provided with jewellery.

Although Burma possesses no diamond mines, it has undoubtedly been a gem country from early times. The regalia of the Burmese court displayed at the South Kensington Museum in London, encrusted and coruscant with rubies set one against the other, row upon row, must be seen to get an idea of how rich in gems was the small kingdom of Burma. Its rubies, sapphires and jade are unrivalled in the world. Jade has been worked since the thirteenth century, but unlike the transparent gem stones, it has not been highly prized by the Burmese people, who call it, merely, *kyauksein,* green-rock. Almost all is sent to China, in valuable quantity and quality, from the tract round the Kachin Hills in Northern Burma, near the town of Mogaung, where, as "the magic powers of heaven and earth are ever combined to form perfect results; so the pure essences of hill and water became solidified into precious jade."

If jade is green-rock, the ruby is red-rock, but it is also *bad-amya,* gem, jewel, possession of highest worth. The ruby mines at Mogok have given the world the Burma ruby, famous among these rare precious stones which vary from deep crimson or purple to pale rose. Here also are found precious sapphires, the two lying in crystalline beds flashed with mica and embedded also with garnets and spinels of all colors, which the poorer people can use for their let-wut let-sa, set in silver, if they cannot buy gold, from the silver mines at Bawdwin about 50 miles away. An ordinary family like ours, with children for whom an expensive modern education is provided, possesses only the "utility" pieces for each member of the family, *i.e.*, the buttons, chains, bangles, rings and ear studs; and a hairpin and comb for the eldest, but this is considered as being poor in let-wut let-sa for a family of our standing. It can be imagined then what good housewives Burmese women have to be. A relative of mine who began petty trading as a young girl was wearing in her middle age diamond rings, one of which held a single stone with the base a little over half-an-inch in diameter. But this can be done with less self-denial than it sounds, because all Burmese people have the same foods and ways of enjoyment, and a man does not develop more expensive habits or likings when he grows richer.

The financial help given to relatives is a part of our family system. It is difficult for nations whose sons go out to work in foreign lands and whose boarding houses contain old fathers and mothers waited on by paid labor, to realize the strong family unity that still exists among nations like the Burmese. Even the naming of relationships knits them together: cousins become "brother-one-womb-removed;" my father's first cousin is my uncle, and his children and we are sisters-two-wombs-removed. The adoption of connections by marriage as one's own is so universally practiced that we children on growing up often meet elders who tell us they are relations, and trace the exact status for us through half a dozen marriages and wombs-removed. Under these circumstances financial help has to cover a great range.

But whereas help to distant relatives may be given out of a sense of a burdensome duty, help to father, mother, brothers and sisters is not regarded as the doing of a favor for which there will be a debt of gratitude. It is expected as the natural order of things. My father saw my two youngest uncles through high school and University, and they, when they were settled, asked to be allowed to see me through my University career although my father did not need help. My Uncle San Lin did so for two years. Now that I am grown up it is my turn to help my younger sisters, and any inheritance which is left will not be touched or the shares assessed until the youngest child has received the same education as the eldest. Our first scholarship money was offered, in the case of every child, to my grandmother as an obeisance and as the highest gift we could offer—earned by learning and dedicated to the eldest person in our lives. When I got my first job and was able to establish my mother in a comfortable suite of rooms, her main emotion was not pleasure at the nice rooms, but a deep joy in saying: "How blessed is my daughter, that she can give material blessings to her mother in her old age, through her own good fortune and merit."

chapter 5

Visits at Grandmother's—New Year festival—Buddhist teach-ings—robberies—floods—elopements

My mother, who had strict ideas about keeping her household a neat family unit of father, mother and children, without de-pendent aunts and other relatives, had equally strong views about the maintenance of our family ties and traditions, especially as we were now having a Western upbringing in the English schools and not many counteracting lessons at home. Once a year at least, she thought, we should go to have the roots of our begin-nings stirred and kept alive. When the younger children were old enough to travel easily, therefore, we went away for each summer vacation.

For her own home, my mother thought a short visit would suffice; the longer visit was paid to my father's family because he could never come with us to see them. In any case, the visits to Thaton were dull for children in those growing-up days; all my mother's family, like herself, had gone into a more worldly life and were settled in their respective professions. The main part of the great house was shut up and empty, and my mother took us there just for a few days to see my aunt, pay a visit to the hpongyi, and to inspect rubber estates which we had just outside Thaton. Then we journeyed on to Ye, where my father's family were still living the life he had planned for them when he worked to buy my grandmother her plots of paddy-land.

Our visits to Ye were pure delight. In childhood any change in itself makes a holiday, and the change from our district life to the life at Ye was very great indeed.

A railway had been built from Moulmein to Ye in 1925; it ended at Ye, where passengers travelling further crossed the creek and continued in buses for about 100 miles of mountain road to Tavoy. This was the only overland route to the Tenasserim coast below Ye. We crossed the Martaban-Moulmein ferry in the early morning, ate breakfast with friends while waiting for the connection, and arrived at Ye about five in the evening. Ye was by then the headquarters of a township and had a population of about 2,000. It was an extremely congested little town, for the number of its houses and inhabitants had just multiplied without any great changes in its original plan or acreage. The two main streets ran parallel to the creek, and along them the Talaing houses were packed, with only three to four feet of space between every few houses to give access from creek to road and from one road to another. The houses were all built on the same pattern, but some were taller, wider and of better quality wood and thatch than others.

Facing the street in line, each house had a verandah running all along its face, and one step took you up from this into the main room of the house. As you entered, this room extended right up to the roof, which sloped very steeply down to its eaves, but about twelve feet in, where the roof was just high enough, a platform upper story was built, looking over a balustrade into the main room below. This platform story ended where the sloping roof again became too low at the back. The back portion reaching to the height of the roof was used for kitchen and washing rooms. But this time, in the row of houses containing ours, the ground had sloped down to the creek, and the kitchen was continued as a bamboo platform raised high above the mud on piles.

Grandmother, who had become among the wealthiest in the village, had made enlargements and adaptations within these lines. Her house was wider, with the clearing up of an adjacent house. It contained four door spaces in its face, each door space throughout the village being a uniform seven feet in width. The main floor was of fine polished teak boards, the part below the platform story was walled off into a bedroom which was very badly ventilated and lighted, the back portion was cleared of all washing rooms and made into a large airy kitchen about thirty feet square, and the platform behind was extended right over the water's edge because we had bought a mooring site further up. On this bamboo platform two hatches were put as bathrooms, containing commodes in the European style, whereas other households walked to the common latrines in the first clearing beyond the street.

The people of Ye lived chiefly by the produce of their gardens, the richer ones like Grandmother sending out to big towns their durians, coconuts, areca nuts, or fish and oysters from the sea, the poorer ones vending fish and vegetables daily around the town, making thatch roofing out of *dani* (nipah) leaves, acting as boatmen up and down the creek, helping to work the gardens and paddy-fields of other families.

My grandmother's household during these years consisted of herself, two aunts, one widow and one spinster, an uncle next to my father in age, my young Uncle Pyant and various cousins, one, two and three wombs removed from us. My elder uncle, Uncle Thet Hnan, had never been out of Ye; after going through the monastery he had worked in the garden instead of going to an English-teaching school. It gave us an uncanny feeling to see him so like my father in build and general appearance and so dissimilar from him in speech, thought and habits. He now owned gardens up at Chaung-bya, and had five children, all of whom had been brought up in Ye. My three boy cousins had been sent to stay with us at various times and were sent to schools which taught English, but nothing would persuade them to take any interest in studies. My cousin Nyein Maung, whom I liked very much, could never bear to keep a shirt on, which was why he was always to be found with only a longyi tucked around his loins playing chinlon or helping boatmen with their canoes, when he should have been sitting fully clothed in a classroom.

My young Uncle Pyant, whom we called U-Ngè, small Uncle, had passed his B.A. and his law degree, and returned to Ye in preference to a more modern life in a larger town. He walled off one doorway's space from the main room of the house and filled it with bookcases, a big desk and chairs for visitors. Outside this room my Uncle Pyant put up a sign saying: *"A-htet tan shaynay gyi:* Advocate and Higher Grade Pleader," and within a very short time became the lawyer of the whole village; but so great was his attachment to this consultation-living-room, which had nothing in common with the rest of Ye, that he relinquished all cases whose developing complexities led client and lawyer to a higher court in Moulmein.

Grandmother had gardens about ten miles up the creek from Ye. These contained coconuts, durians and areca nuts grown over about fifty acres for commercial disposal. Around the bungalow in the center of the garden there grew mangosteen, rambutan, pomeloes and pineapples for eating on a large scale, clumps of bamboos, a coffee tree, tobacco plants, capsicum, lime and citron trees, lemon grass, and vegetables of all kinds to serve the needs of the bungalow and the household in town. My aunts with one young male relative took turns to live at the garden and help the family that was hired to look after it permanently. It was a dangerous life in these plantations as dacoities were very frequent. The produce was taken down to Ye in a succession of graceful narrow boats shaped out of single tree trunks. The durians and

coconuts were sold straight away to traders who travelled between Moulmein and Ye for this purpose. The areca nuts were
first dried on a bamboo attic made by an extension of the platform upper story of the house until it met the back slope of the
roof. When they were dried the whole family gathered around
in the back kitchen and removed the husks with blunted nutcrackers, leaving the smooth nut to be sold.

With the rice from the paddy-land on the opposite bank, fruits,
vegetables and spices from the garden, rolling their cheroots with
a mixture containing tobacco in leaves shed by the areca trees in
the garden, and grinding their own coffee berries, my aunts and
grandmother only needed to buy a little fish and meat for their
daily consumption. This they could not provide themselves owing
to the Buddhist law against taking life. Only the hardened ones
of the village, *ta-nga-thès*, drew and netted in the wealth of fish
around Ye, and the theoretical condemnation in which their profession was held absolved all good Buddhists from any sin in
eating the fruits of their labors.

My aunts bought vast quantities of fish for salting and drying.
This cured fish supplied our yearly needs as well as theirs. They
also bought prawns to press into a paste called *ngapi*, in this
case *seinsa* ngapi, which forms the basis of all our flavoring and
condiments. As soon as the ta-nga-thè came up with his boat-
loads of prawns they were spread out on rough bamboo mats
and sunned on the big platform behind the house. When they
were fairly dried, my aunts, with a helper or two from the village,
mashed up the prawns by hand, throwing in vast quantities of
salt as they worked. The mess was left in the sun for a few days,
being stirred every now and again. By this time it had turned
into a grey-black paste, more or less smooth, smelling most pungent and rotten to foreigners but *hmway-dè*, fragrant, to us, and
tasting like a concentrate of anchovy. This paste is stored in small
glazed earthenware jars. It is used to flavor all meat and vegetable dishes, or is fried or pounded with other ingredients to provide condiments for the meal. The Tenasserim coast is the chief

source of seinsa ngapi in Burma, the big towns of Tavoy and Mergui supplying towns in Upper Burma as well. The large amounts of salt needed come from the valuable salt fields in this area, which produce about 6,000 tons annually.

It can be imagined what excitement a holiday at Ye caused us in our growing years, and even my mother's admonitions that we were to behave in accordance with the strict Burmese ideas which prevailed at Ye rather than the un-Burmese habits acquired at school did not dampen our excitement. We were then at English-speaking schools, where we had adopted the habit of calling each other by name. The eldest of my young sisters, Mya Mya, is seven years younger than I am, but when she went to school I had only two sisters left who called me respectfully, *Ma-Ma Gyi,* elder sister, and by the time the youngest was at school there was no Ma-Ma Gyi left in the family. The tradition of the younger ones fetching and carrying for the elder had also sadly deteriorated.

At meals, my mother had not kept up the custom of helping the eldest person present with a portion of every dish before it was open to the rest of the company. Before we went to Ye, therefore, my mother gathered us around her and told us how we were to behave so as to give our grandmother and aunts great pleasure in our visit and no rude shocks. "Now don't forget, *the-mi-to,* my daughters, you will all three call your sister Big-Elder-Sister; you, Pusu, are to call Mya Mya Middle-Elder-Sister, and Aye Little-Elder-Sister. In fact you should always do so, at home and everywhere else, but mother understands that you make habits easily at your English school. Never walk into the house with your slippers on, as you do in the downstairs room here. When you eat with your grandmother and aunts, don't touch anything until your aunts have put a little of it into Grandmother's plate. And try not to talk to one another in English." All the way in the train my sisters would fling themselves at me and shout, "Big Elder Sister, Big Big Elder Sister."

We went to Ye during our summer holidays, which were the

longest in the school year, and allowed us three weeks with my father and a month at Ye. It also enabled us to pay obeisance to our grandmother at the New Year, and to celebrate this loveliest of festivals in its most fitting surroundings. My Uncle San Lin usually sent his wife and our four small cousins at the same time, so that for one month in the year at least Grandmother could feel that the world of big towns and English civilization had not robbed her of any family affection. Sleeping and eating arrangements for the gathering of twenty-odd people were no problems for the simple large-scale economy of the household. My mother had a bed, and beside it my Aunt Khin and all the children slept on thinbyus laid side by side on the platform upper story. Meals were eaten in successive rounds at a low table on the kitchen floor, not served as separate sittings, but by calling more diners as places were vacated, and filling each dish that diminished from the stove near-by.

Half of our visit to Ye was spent at the garden, where we were surrounded by rich fruits and could bathe in the clear swift water that rushed through islands of reeds. We walked and rode in bullock carts for miles, to visit other gardens owned by Grandmother's friends—old men and women who lived there all the time, and who chuckled with delight to see us, for to them we were not ourselves, not ordinary children like those playing about them. We were ready-made reproductions sent back by my father and Uncle San Lin, who disappeared into an unknown world many years ago. At house after house, and at the same houses year after year, we sat in a row on the benches they kept on the verandahs of all houses, eight children awkward and restrained, while the old people peered and chuckled at us: "Yes, that is San Lin, all right—but there is Htwa Yin's nose; look at this expression, it is Maung Chit Khaing himself—oh but look here, here is the image of Maung Pyant, yes, exactly Maung Pyant, hullo you little Pyant, oh, look at her." This was my poor sister Mya Mya, whose face seemed to be the quintessence of the features of my father and all his brothers and sisters. My sister Aye and I, who had the good fortune to take after my mother's family, were noticed very little during these visits, but my poor little Mya Mya sat there solemn and unhappy, thrusting her face out until even to us she looked comically like the forty-year-old aunts and uncles.

When I think back on eating the fruits of Grandmother's garden, they seem to have the quality of some heavenly ambrosia about them. They were all such luscious fruits. For example, the durian, the fruit which foreigners describe as smelling most foul, usually had in Rangoon only a thin layer of the precious golden flesh around the seeds. In this garden we ate only *shwe-dinga* durians, golden-sovereign durians, whose flesh was so soft and full that a gold coin could be stood on edge on the seed and be buried in it. Moreover, the eating of durians in excess was usually discouraged anywhere else, because of the heating qualities of the fruit, but here they grew beside the cooling mangosteen, which we always ate after the durian. This delicious fruit never travels successfully; even from district to district it gets bruised and stained.

The mangosteen tree was most exciting to me as a child. It was full of dark foliage and the distilled nectar of the snow-white fruit seemed to be enclosed in bitterness and fraught with dangers, its stain was indelible and to be kept carefully away from our clothes, and the fruit itself was said to be poisonous when eaten with sugar. This was owing to the belief that the sap of the rind made a toxic combination with sugar. Even the coconuts in Ye had a succulence about them. They were so abundant in the garden that we discarded all the fruit in which the meat had hardened beyond the *zun-chit*, the "spoon-scrape," stage, when the flesh was of such tenderness that it could be scraped up with a spoon as a transparent jelly, to be put into the drink of coconut water. We were encouraged to drink this because it was said to make the heat "kick" and come out of the system. The grains of the pomeloes also were swollen and pink with juice; we shredded them in piles and ate them with prawn powder and fish sauce.

94

The *kanazo,* the *baccaurea sapida,* gave us a fruit of a mouth-watering sweet-sourness. This fruit was said to induce diarrhea and we were always made to eat the white piths, which had a binding action.

Whereas we feasted on the fruits of trees, our elders turned to the sea for more fleshly succulence. My mother and aunts loved to get turtles' eggs, nastily soft white things the size of golf balls, boil them and tear them open to spill their richness on to a plate of boiled rice; they got oysters swimming soft and cold in vinegar; big nga-tha-lauk, hilsa fish, bursting with fatness, and thick buffalo's milk, which always seemed to us more meaty and strong than cow's milk.

We came back to Ye itself for the New Year festival. The New Year in our lunar calendar usually occurs round about April 13th, and is the occasion of the descent of a spirit-king, the Tha-gya Min, king of the tha-gyas, from heavenly regions to the world of men. The Burman Buddhist idea of the universe places the hellish, the earthly and the heavenly regions in well-defined order. In the center of the universe is Mount Myinmo, the highest peak in all the world, a million miles above the sea and a million below the waters. Round about the sides of this mountain are ranged the six levels of heavenly regions where the Dewas or heavenly spirits dwell. These heavenly spirits also have homes in the sun, moon and stars. Far up in the heavens, above the seats of the Dewas, are ranged the sixteen seats of more perfect beings, the Byammas, one above the other. And far above them, as high as the imagination can soar, are four sublime seats, on the borders of the supreme Nirvana.

Below the six levels of the Dewa regions of Myinmo are seven ranges of mountains, girdling the earth in a perfect ring interposed only by seven seas. In these seas are set four great islands, to the north, south, east and west of Myinmo Mountain, each attended by five hundred small islands grouped around it. On each island grows a fabulous tree which gives its name to the island, and there dwell beings whose heads are shaped like the shape of the island. The northern, eastern and western islands are all more fair than the southern, life lasts for five hundred or a thousand years, and the trees bear gorgeous dresses and delicious foods of meat, but the inhabitants of the southern islands are infinitely more blessed in their merit.

This island of Zampudipa, shaped like a trapezium and bearing the Zampu tree, surrounded by five hundred islands where live the English and the other nations of the human world, is the abode of man, the Buddhist man, and the known neighbors who are heretics from Buddhism. Here the inhabitants must work to weave their clothes and cook their food and live perhaps at the most a hundred years, but here also, and only here, do the Buddhas appear to teach the right way of living, which is the only way in which the people can progress to the heavenly regions and to Nirvana. Down below the earth are situated the hells, eight great ones and forty thousand and forty smaller hells, regions of torture and punishment.

Whereas the inhabitants of the northern, eastern and western islands around Myinmo, never hearing the words of a Buddha and never knowing the way of good and evil, are always born into the same world, never going up or down, man, the inhabitant of Zampudipa, may pass into the nethermost hell or the highest heavenly seat, according to the progress in his successive lives. Ascending the ladder from deep hells, through earth to heavenly regions, the spirit meets with existences which are not only more blessed in the degree of enjoyment and material happiness, but also correspondingly more free from fleshly desires and sin.

Our Buddhist hells are the most frightening places one can imagine; as a child I used to look at the vivid pictures drawn in the friezes round pagoda building walls, to show the damnation that would befall the evildoer who was born into a hell. Boiling in oil, flesh being torn off the bones by monstrous dogs and vultures, saws and knives aflame with red heat slowly dismembering limb from limb, all these occur in life in any of the hells. The next stage upwards from hell is a life as an animal, which a man may

96

be born to for lesser sins and an omission from doing meritorious deeds. Animals have their stages of nobility also. Lowest are those living on excrements of flesh of other animals, nobler are the herbivorous animals and noblest of all the elephant. Gautama Buddha passed one of his existences as a white elephant, which is the reason for the esteem in which a white elephant was held— so high, that Buddhist kings longed to be able to style themselves, *Hsin-byu Shin*, Lord (Owner) of the white elephant.

During his life as a man, a being had the opportunity to live a right life, observing the precepts, giving alms and attending the pagoda regularly. His next existence might then be as an inhabitant of one of the six seats of the Dewas. In all these six seats through which the being may progress, life is surrounded by delights of foods, clothing and dwelling, but passion is less sensual, and decreases with ascent. Successively, a touch of the hand, and then gazing at the lover, and finally the mere presence in the same existence is enough to satisfy love. From here, concentrated meditation will carry a being higher to the seats of the Byammas; here he must get rid of all remaining affection for matter, for all parts of the body, until he attains to the four seats of Arupa. The contempt for matter continues in these existences, and finally, when all false persuasions leave the spirit, he passes into Nirvana, the lifeless, timeless state of bliss, in which the spirit knows no joy and no sorrow, but remains perpetually contemplating the abstract truth, delivered finally from the cycle of recurring existences.

This arrangement of the universe and of the progress of man through different levels of it was but a reflection of the Buddhist ideas of cosmography prevalent at the time when the religion was first in flower. In our imagination they belonged with the distant Himalayas, the peaks too high for human sight, the clouds and mist on which a being with the Buddha's spiritual powers could ride in majesty. But whether every Burman Buddhist associates these regions with his daily life or not, there are few who, in the midst of their busiest worldly living, will not be excited, exalted, at the Canonical descriptions of the mind of the *arahat* when he becomes, by meditation and victory over the senses, ready to attain Nirvana. The following description is part of the Sammannaphala-sutta, one of the discourses of the Buddha:

"With mind concentrated, purified, cleansed, spotless, with the defilements gone, supple, ready to act, firm, impassible, he directs his attention to knowledge and insight. He understands that this my body has a shape, consists of the four elements, was produced by a mother and father, a collection of milk and gruel, subject to rubbing, pounding, breaking, and dissolution, and on this my consciousness rests, hereto it is bound.

"He then directs his attention to creating a mind-formed body. From his body he creates a mind-formed body having shape, and with all its limbs and faculties.

"He directs his attention to various kinds of magical powers. From being one he becomes many, and from being many becomes one. He goes across walls and hills without obstruction, plunges into and out of the earth, goes over water as if on dry land, passes through the air sitting cross-legged, and even touches the mighty moon and sun with his hand, and reaches to the world of Brahma.

"With purified divine ear he hears divine and human sounds both distant and near.

"He understands the state of the minds of other beings.

"The last three stages he attains are called the knowledges.

"First, the monk directs his attention to remembering his former existences. He remembers thousands of births and many cycles of existence, and knows that in such a place he was a being of such a name and clan, and had certain experiences and length of life in each of these births.

"Second, he directs his attention to the knowledge of the passing away and rebirth of beings. With divine purified vision he sees evil-doers being reborn in hell, and the virtuous in heaven, just as a man in a palace may see persons entering and coming out of a house.

98

New Year festival

"Third, he directs his attention to the knowledge of the destruction of the asavas [desires and impulses, expressions of the clinging to existence]. He duly understands, 'this is pain,' 'this is the cause of pain,' 'this is the cessation of pain,' 'this is the way leading to the cessation of pain.' He duly understands, 'these are the asavas,' 'this is the cause of the asavas,' 'this is the cessation of the asavas,' 'this is the way to the cessation of the asavas.' When he thus knows and thus perceives, his mind is released from the asava of lust, from the asava of [desire for] existence, from the asava of ignorance. In the released is the knowledge of his release; he understands that rebirth is destroyed, the religious life has been led, done is what was to be done, there is nothing further beyond this world."

At the New Year, then, the King of the tha-gyas, who are Dewas, comes to visit the earth, which is suffering its hottest and driest month and looks to rain and coolness for deliverance. Before the descent each year, Brahmins and astrologers get together and calculate the exact hour of his arrival, the means of his descent to the earth, whether astride a buffalo, a *naga* or a *galon*, and whether he wields a spear or a water jar, for by these signs will the nature of the coming year be decided—heavy rains or drought, good crops or disturbances in the land—and the duration of his stay on the earth. All their findings are collected in leaflets which are distributed as the *tha-gyan sa*, and when I was young I used to think that they fell from heaven as prophetic messages. Actually the present-day practice is to fix April 13th for the official occurrence of Thingyan each year. The celebration of the festival by pouring of water is to honor the heavenly visitor, to wash away the old year's dirtiness and to begin the new by good and auspicious deeds.

By the day before Tha-gya Min's arrival in Ye, the *a-kyo nay,* the preparing-to-greet day, bamboo palisades had been put up along the verandahs, arrangements had been made for communal celebration and large-scale washing and feeding. All the girls spent the morning grinding thanakha and other fragrant barks and the boys went out to cut the leaves of the *the-byay* tree for the sacred water pots to be poured out at the arrival of the visitor. In the evening, Grandmother and other old people walked up to the rest houses near the monastery where my father had been educated, for at their time of life, fasting, meditation and the contemplation of younger people's enjoyment is the happiest way of greeting the New Year. In the evening, too, we carried out Grandmother's good deed of inviting a number of people from the village to come and wash their hair. Hairwashing is part of the New Year's rituals because the noblest part of the body, the head, must be in a clean condition at this time. In the days of the Burmese kings, there was a ceremonial washing of the King's hair at the New Year, called the *tha-gyan daw gyi*. The water was always brought from the clear springs of *Gaung-se kyun,* the island lying dark and green in the Moulmein river. The island had a special sanctity because it was believed to hang suspended from the heavens by an invisible cord. When the island passed into British territory after the first Burmese war, however, the waters of Gaung-se kyun were no longer used for this sacred purpose, and substitute clear water was got from the Irrawaddy.

Burmese people wash their hair with the alkaline juices of the bark of a tree known as *tha-yaw*, combined with the seeds of the *accacia concina*. The bark, which is stored in a dried condition, is soaked for a few hours before washing, the accacia seeds are boiled in their pods until they are soft and are then crushed into the tha-yaw water. The result is a slippery mixture which we still use in preference to modern shampoos on the market. The provision of this in basins, and of clear water in big jars on our bamboo platform, was considered a meritorious act on New Year's eve. About twenty people came, bringing towels and a change of clothing. They washed their hair and bathed on the bamboo platform over the creek. The ladies put thanakha thickly on their cheeks and gave children blobs where the "roses" of English children's cheeks are, and we all sat on the edge of the platform, hair floating free in the breeze, and watched the sun go down. At night we helped to put the ground bark into little cups and stuck tha-byay leaves in the pots and went to bed full of pleasant anticipations. Tha-gya Min usually arrived about midnight, when Uncle Pyant got out his revolver and fired a salute to announce his arrival to the village. My male cousins stayed up to pour the water pots away, but we slept right through this actual arrival.

Early next morning we woke up to find big tubs of water placed on the front verandah. Uncle Pyant gave each child a piston for squirting water, and there was terrific excitement as we chased about the house to greet each other with the first pouring of water. Our maids and dependents always affected great terror at the immodesty of being bathed by great splashes from my male cousins; they shrieked and clambered up ladders in a most unladylike fashion and tried to barricade themselves from the drenching. In the street, too, fun had begun already. Children of about eight years and below were all stripped naked and let loose with their pistons and tubs of water to run and soak each passer-by.

But in the kitchens of the houses aunts and mothers were busy dishing out the morning meal to be sent up to the *zayat*, where grandmothers keeping the fast would eat only this one meal of the day. My cousin Ma Aye Shwe and the dependent girls put on their brightest clothes of washable materials and set the trays on their heads. All the houses did likewise and the procession collected more girls as it passed each house on its way towards the zayats. Behind the girls, the young lads of the village followed with empty tins and buckets, to go and draw water with which to bathe the images of the Buddha, and then the bath water for the old folk in the zayat. The procession always looked very gay, for the girls wore stout bright cotton prints instead of the usual white muslin jackets, so that the wet clinging clothes after a splashing would not make immodest figures of them. As this procession passed, not even the naughtiest urchin would dare to splash them as long as they headed in the direction of the monastery. Arrived at their destination, the young people served the meal to the elders, drew the water and washed the images, filled the jars with bath water for their grandmothers, ate their own meal from the pooled remains of what they had brought, and then started uproarious fun. The young men had the advantage of their buckets, but the girls had the advantage of being able to use guile by affecting fear and helplessness until they could turn the buckets round on their pursuers. After this they went in search of the ngu branches, the equivalent, in Ye, of the *padauk* flowers which boys and girls in other parts of Burma were plucking.

The padauk is the *pterocarpus indica,* a tall tree growing in the mixed dry forests of Burma and giving a rich red wood which is much used in the making of bullock carts. It is also a beautiful flowering tree, whose bright yellow blossoms are always associated with the freshness of the New Year festivities, for it flowers at this time and its branches are cut down and dragged into houses with drops of water lighting up the golden yellow flowers against the rich dark green leaves, either water from the water throwers or the *tha-gyan mo,* the thingyan showers. Light showers usually fall about this time although the monsoon is far off yet; they come from a small low pressure area over the land, although when we were young it seemed to be part of what the true tha-gyan-sa leaflets should promise, a foretaste of the coolness of the real monsoon, and a recognition of Tha-gya Min's presence. If the rain was late in falling, the villagers set to work to hurry it on. The rain spirits live in the stars but they sometimes come out to play with each other in the space of the firmament. Then rain falls on the earth. But at other times, when the sun is not in the right quarter, they stay indoors and the earth receives only the scorching heat of the sun. Men can then rouse the rain spirits to show more energy and come out, by the beating of tin cans and by exerting energy themselves in a tug-of-war. In Ye, the upper street and the lower street used to put up teams for this and tugging was carried on amidst betting and cheering and the beating of empty kerosene tins by women and children around.

The girls and youths from the monastery returned at about noon, wet and happy and dragging the branches of *ngu* along. Throughout the day the children ran into the street to pour water on passers-by; bullock carts went by, decorated with ngu branches and holding music and water parties of young men and girls, the young men richly painted and dancing in the open carts; rival teams drew up and staged water-fights in the street or went to besiege houses where beautiful girls with a reputation for coldness or coyness were hiding. Throughout the day, also, dishes of sweetmeats arrived, for each house does the good act of making a comestible in large quantities for distribution. Ours was made on the second day and was a Moulmein specialty for which my mother had the best talent.

This *tha-gyan hta-min,* thingyan rice, sounds insipid when described as boiled rice, eaten floating in cold water which has been made fragrant, to the accompaniment of green mango salad and salt fish shredded and fried crisp. To us, of course, it is delicious. The water has received an infusion of the aroma from an earthen pot which is turned upside down over the burning of tallow and fragrant woods. The rice is not the moist steamy rice of meal times but has been drained after cooking, on tray-sieves of cane, and the grains lie clear and separate and whole. The delight of eating thingyan rice in the hot weather is indescribable to foreigners, perhaps even to all non-Moulmein people, eating it in wide china bowls, with china spoons, alternating the concentration of sour and salt tastes of mango and salt fish with the coolness and cleanness of the rice and its water. We could eat this throughout the day; being thingyan rice it carried a blessedness which made us immune to stomach ache, in the same way as it would be graceless to think that one could catch cold from the playing of thingyan water.

During the three days of the festival communal celebrations were also carried on, with shows and free feasting every night at pandals put up by each section of the streets. By the *a-tetnay*, rising day, when the Tha-gya Min goes back to the heavenly regions, everyone was a bit worn out, but the more energetic spirits declared that Tha-gya Min had forgotten his pipe or umbrella and had come back for one day more to fetch it. People try not to tell lies, quarrel, swear or lose their tempers during the days of the New Year. Apart from the offence it would give to the ears of the heavenly visitor in the vicinity it was considered a bad omen to begin the new year with such wicked behavior. Children were always warned not to be disobedient in case the Tha-gya Min should note it, but the reason was also that the grown-ups should not be forced to scold them during this period. Woe to the servant maid who blunders then; greater woe indeed for her sin in causing the mistress to scold her and use angry words.

The years saw little change in the social program of our visits to Ye, but in the absence of social changes, the human element always seemed more strong and primitive, and all the drama and romance of which we had so little in our placid district houses was concentrated in Ye. Life there seemed more full of physical movement and danger, anger was more strong, love more sweeping, quarrels more deep and lasting than we were used to. Births, deaths, disease and elopements all seemed to happen more frequently. It was all terror, excitement and romance to us.

A robbery at any of the houses in the village woke the whole quarter up, house by house, as the screams from there were taken up by frightened neighbors. My male cousins and all the men of the village hitched their longyis up around their loins and ran hither and thither in the night, with lanterns in one hand and dahs in the other. The womenfolk, as soon as the men had rushed out to the rescue, barricaded their doors and collected together in a whispering group, lest the fleeing robber should dodge into an open doorway in the shuttered line and demand silence and shelter at the point of his dah. On these occasions when we huddled together already terror-stricken, my grandmother recounted

robberies—ghosts—floods

her story of the time when she failed to shut her door in time, and the robber was in the shadow of it as she went forward to fold it. "Not a word," he said, showing his blade. "Look out and see which way they have gone. Are they there? How many? Is the street clear? Don't talk loud." In this way Grandmother helped the felon to escape.

Once or twice during the day we saw a saung, a blanket like ours except that patches of blood made violent interruptions on the chaste red and white striped design, being slung on a pole, carrying a woman who had been hacked by the dah of a hot-tempered husband. When one of the villagers had died a sudden death through poisoning, we listened wide-eyed to Ma Aye Shwe's account of his burial. All the old and broken bottles of Ye had been collected and ground up. His grave was dug, and after the coffin had been put into it, was filled up with alternating layers of earth and of powdered glass. This was because one of our persisting animist beliefs is that a spirit whose body dies a "green" death, that is, sudden, violent and unnatural, will walk about the earth in the form of an undesirable ghost, and hence the glass which will keep it under the earth and prevent its escape, much as thieves are deterred from climbing a wall which has powdered glass strewn along its top.

Every few years also, the water of the Ye creek rose so high that the ground and main floors of all the houses were flooded, and my grandmother and aunts had to retreat with all perishable goods and furniture to the high reaches of the platform story and camp there until the water retreated. How we longed to visit Ye when this happened, but the nearest we came to realizing these floods was to see unexpected little patches of the sand of the creek every now and again in the houses, where the traces of the visiting waters had not been swept away. In one really bad year the waters at chaung-bya swelled into a mountainous flood which rose suddenly in a great roar and carried with it huts and rafts and stored goods of all kinds. Grandmother and my great-aunts watched dumbly from the top of the pagoda hill, while cocks and hens and dogs and people clung to the thatched roofs of the floating houses, the cocks crowing and dogs baying and people praying, all rushing swiftly and inevitably past Ye, towards the great Thamoddhaya, the great ocean which is part of the waters which break the girdle of the Settkyawala Mountains circling the world around Myinmo Mount. Every few years, as a matter of fact, Uncle Thet Hnan, who had a garden and house at chaung-bya, lost a few tins of sesamum oil, or some part of his bamboo structures. This was because they all built and rebuilt the houses too near the water, to provide a quick escape from dacoits and enemies.

It was a dangerous life in these gardens even during our most recent years there, and my cousin Nyein Maung, who was the stalwart to give my aunts most protection, developed into a rough and ready dispenser of justice. On one occasion he watched the hand of a thief creep up through the bamboo slates of the flooring on which his little son played. The child wore a gold anklet which the hand coming out of the darkness tried to wrench off. Nyein Maung, who anticipated that the thief would soon lose his patience and cut off the troublesome ankle joint, gave a swift and gentle cut at the hand with his own dah, and went on calmly with his work, while the thief, realizing the justice of it, quietly withdrew his hand and fled. To these tucked-away gardens, also, came the deformed and mentally defective members of households, to find a more secluded place from public jeering both of themselves and of their families. We felt sad to see the goiter growths and scarred faces, but as children we joined in with the baiting of old crones whose great accomplishment was to utter automatic and irrelevant imprecations whenever they were dug in the ribs.

A much happier aspect was that in Ye the young people were always eloping. As I grew older I used to wonder that love came so easily and in such unlikely places. A proper elopement must have certain attendant circumstances. Usually the parents do not agree to it, but quite often also the two people are very young

elopements

and feel that love is wicked and is bound to be disapproved of, so they decide to elope. There is always a confidant of the girl's or man's or both, to help with the arrangements for the flight, or for the refuge. The girl usually wraps a few clothes in a small cloth bundle, and from the meeting place the journey to the secret destination is made by canoe, or bullock cart. The disappearance of the girl is soon discovered, the alarm is given, people rush about with exciting news, mother and father make a crying visit to the house of the elder friend and adviser of their or the young man's family, and beat their breasts at the shamelessness and wickedness of the girl. The hidden couple are soon tracked down, a reconciliation takes place and a proper wedding feast is held for the young people. Then the whole disgrace is completely forgotten, until about seventeen years later, when perhaps the daughter of the bride elopes, and her friends commiserating with her tears, shake their heads sadly and say that this is *nga-yé,* the punishment for her own sin of seventeen years before.

chapter 6

My father's retirement—rubber and other crops—rice—
father's prayers—alchemy—the marriage market—duty days
—the old house

MEN of my father's generation followed a definite pattern in the
stages of their lives. They passed their infancy and early childhood playing around their mother's knee, but as soon as they
were capable of receiving spiritual influence and training, the
atmosphere of the monastery and the men of religion enwrapped
them. Thus their spiritual life began at the monastery. After they
left it they spent many stages in the world of offices and money-
earning, but none of them could be reconciled to this as the final
stage of their lives. They hoped to leave this when they were
fifty or soon after, and go back full circle to spending the twi-
light in the atmosphere of religion, before they went out finally
in childish decay to another and better existence. The retirement

108

Thaton, pensioner's paradise

in childish decay to another and better existence. The retirement
from the civil service was therefore a very important point in my
father's life. The English term "pensioner" has come to be incorporated into popular Burmese usage, as *pin-sin tha-ma,* so full
of meaning is it. Most men at this time look about for a town
which will ensure easy living and performance of meritorious
deeds, in which to settle down. We went back to Thaton because
of our family connections, but, as it happened, Thaton was also
the most noted town in Burma for the settling of pin-sin tha-mas;
it was indeed the pensioner's paradise.

Thaton is a very old town. From the fifth to the tenth century
A.D. it flourished as the center of a Buddhist kingdom of Talaings,
while the greater Burmese capital at Pagan was still without the
true faith. There the Burmese King and the people were under
the sway of a body of monks called the Aris, whose hypnotic influence was exercised through the practice of ritualistic observances contrary to the teachings of the Buddha and of which they
set themselves to be the high priests. To this capital came a
Buddhist monk from Thaton called Shin Arahan. He came into
the presence of the King with his staff and a simple robe and the
stamp of an ascetic life on his face, but also with the serene
assurance that a monk's life ennobled any man beyond all other
men, for he went up to the throne of the King and sat upon it.
King Anawrahta asked, "What is the true teaching of this holy
religion, and where can one get its Books?" Shin Arahan then
told the King of the Buddhist kingdom of Thaton and the sacred
scriptures which were there. The King of Pagan sent messengers
to Thaton for copies of the scriptures, but the proud King at
Thaton would not yield them. The Burmese King thereupon went
down with an army which succeeded in carrying off King, clergy
and scriptures from the unfortunate city of Thaton. King Ma-
nuha of Thaton languished on a throne seat of bare stone in
Pagan, but the religion thrived and blossomed into the grandeur
of the thousand pagodas and temples of Pagan, so that even today Burmans can see the white majesty of the Ananda and re-

joice in the way their kings received and enshrined their faith.

With king and religion transplanted, Thaton fell into a decline, and soon lost her trade also, for the seacoast extended and left Thaton a dry inland town. However, it never lost its reputation as the old seat of religion; its rich geographical features also re-mained—a soil which can grow rice, fruits and plantations of other crops in abundance; its easy access to the big towns of Moulmein and Rangoon; the Martaban Hills, which were ranged behind the town, and over which waterfalls tumbled down to cross the red laterite roads as streams of clear water.

Most pensioners, by the time they retired, had already estab-lished some form of livelihood other than the drawing of their pension. My father owned two rubber plantations just outside Thaton, each about 110 acres. Burma is not one of the chief rubber-producing areas of the world, but the country round Tenasserim is suitable for rubber-growing and produced the greater part of what was, in 1939, a total of over 22,000,000 pounds. Thaton district contained about 15,628 acres of rubber, between big planters and many small plantations like ours.

My parents started our estates in the form of clearings which they planted with the help of my grandfather in about 1910, before my father became a myook, and were in time to reap the riches of the great boom in the post-war years, when they were selling rubber at Rs. 2/-° per pound and my father bought a motor boat and my mother many diamonds. As a Government servant my father was not allowed to work at any trade, so he handed over the possession of the estates to my mother's sister, our Kyi-Kyi Lon, who all her spinster life has devoted herself to my mother and to us. She worked the estates for us and, in the awful years of the slump that followed, we quite forgot indeed that we owned any such things as rubber plantations, for the only connection which my father ever had with them, the receipt of money from Kyi-Kyi, disappeared completely.

° Two rupees, no annas. The rupee contains 16 annas. Shortly before World War II the Burmese rupee was worth around 37 cents.

rubber plantations

In 1935, however, when my father retired, the market for rubber had just begun to stir into being. The Burma Rubber Committee allowed planters like us an annual quota of about 20,000 pounds or two-thirds of our production, which we hoped to sell at roughly 7 annas per pound, and my father was free to work them again. He had no technical knowledge and the minimum amount of business acumen, and I never ceased to wonder how money could come to us in this haphazard way. We kept a manager and his family in the bungalow of each plantation, and a staff of eight or nine tappers. Once a week we drove out there on a picnic inspection; my father and mother gazed with pride on the rows of neat trees, walked right round to see that clearings were maintained and that the trees looked right, peered into the cups of rich white latex, administered rebukes and instructions and inspected the books, visited the smoking house and saw the brown smoked sheets with GK stamped on them, after the traditional Burmese way of married business—G for Gyi, my mother, and K for Khaing, my father—and then we all returned home. Chinese traders came to the house and while chewing betel they talked about quantities and prices of the stock we had. Then the stacked sheets came from the plantation in the two bullock carts which we kept there, and the traders came and took them away and paid us in cash. Business was something so foreign to what we had always seen our parents doing, and this all seemed so simple, that we always felt they were surely being cheated.

Some of the other pensioners did not believe in dabbling with commodities that depended on a world market. Even the way in which we grew rubber went too much into the world of specialized commerce which might have pitfalls for a retired civil servant. A friend of my father's grew large gardens of *da-nyin*, a tree of the laburnum species. The fruit of this tree rivals the durian for its nauseating effect on foreign sensibilities. It does not exude a smell as the durian does, until you eat it, but after eating it the smell comes out in breath, sweat and all other excretions. But it is one of our favorite foods. It is a small flat circular fruit of a hard and smooth consistency, enclosed in a shell which prises open in neat halves like an oyster shell. The texture and taste are delicious. We boil or bake it as a vegetable for fish sauce, we salt it in big jars as a pickle, we beat it and make it swim in coconut milk and eat it as a sweet, we bury it and make it sprout into a more pungent form called *da-nyin wet.* The main point is that it is eaten in vast quantities. It also contains substances which are good for diabetics, and families buy it literally in hundreds. No world depression interferes with the demand for *da-nyin thi,* and though the sale price is low, overhead charges are almost nil.

Other families in Thaton got their extra income from paddy-land. Although the rice for which Burma is so famous today did not enter world markets till the latter half of the last century, the possession of *lè,* fields, which is synonymous with paddy-fields, is a well-established form of wealth. Our part of Burma is particularly rich in fields. Nearly all the 3,500,000 tons of rice which is exported annually from Burma comes from Lower Burma, where Tenasserim Division ranks among the three most productive areas, and Thaton district takes first place in Tenasserim. But rice is more than the chief export crop of the country to us. It is our *wun-sa,* food for the womb, our staple food; and we have depended so much on it that we pay it reverence, almost. When we were young, A-Kyi and our nurses never allowed us to tread on any rice that had been spilt; rice was like a master and human beings its servants, they said. The phrase for "I was not born yesterday" is "I grew up eating rice," and in the same way excessive stupidity excites wonder that the person nourished on rice can be so stupid. Through years of journeying on trains, bullock carts, and river steamers, we have seen the peaceful green fields, the dry reaped rice, the golden grain heaped on small canoes before milling. Though we did not know the toil and the uncertain hopes of the cultivators, we followed the growth of the life-giving grain through all its stages, seeing the first sproutings in one place in one year, the ripe and mature crop in another, and the thriving young stalks of a later generation at another place and time.

Our fields seemed perpetually marked into small beds by ridges six inches high. Lying empty during the first months of the year, these beds grew parched and baked by April and May. With the first blessed showers of the monsoon about mid-May, however, one, two, three, four or more inches of rain fell on the beds within about ten days, and softened the hard crust. Men went to work about the end of the month, and with harrow and plough they chopped and churned up the earth, cutting and burying weeds, refining the rough, and making the stiff clay soil pliant until a soft fine mud was produced. In the meantime, the seeds had been soaked in water in deep layers between banana leaves, to make them sprout and become more receptive of the soil's richness. These were brought out in baskets, and young men and women, wearing wide bamboo hats in the heavy showers, walked about scattering them, using up to ten basketfuls in one acre. They allowed the seeds to lie for a few days and then let in a gentle amount of water to flood the beds—one or two inches now, and more and more as the plants grew taller. In the meantime, vast stretches of beds were being prepared in the same way—plough and harrow and chop the weeds which here had become bigger and rougher with the rains, but would feed the soil better for that reason. When they had finished, all the countryside along the railway line looked like a vast segmented mirror, all the fine mud of the field lying beneath the four inches of water, and not a green weed to be seen.

By now the plants in the nursery beds were about one and a half to two feet tall, and it was mid-July. Men plucked the seedlings, tying them swiftly into bundles of about 750. They chopped off the heads to free the plant of leaves which might make the young stalks topple over when they were planted upright. Then men and women stood ankle deep in the main beds and with one deft stroke of the right hand they planted two or four stalks straight into the soft mud, each group a few inches from the next. It was this long and laborious task which gave the Lower Burman his landscape of endless green fields of rich waving paddy. From now on, these fields had only to be tended with water, neither to be stagnant, flooded, nor too dry. Through the months of September and October the rains diminished, the soil grew drier and the grain ripened from green to yellow. In December it was cut, tied in bundles and sunned for further drying and carried to the threshing floor. Here the bundles were ranged in rows with ears turned inwards, on the hardened surface of mud and dung, and bullocks trod round and round on them, slow and confident that their heavy hoofs would crush the chaff and leave the hard grain whole; and lo! when the mixture of corn and chaff was handed up in baskets to a high platform and tumbled down in a strong wind, the wind blew the chaff and dust away, but the rice fell in a clean heap on the ground below.

Thus cultivators, and the weeds, earth, rain, sun, oxen and wind produced our wun-sa; but alas, the bounding broadcast sower, the slim, red-skirted deft-handed transplanters and the loving water-layers of this description were too often merely tenants or hired workers on the land. Owing to various causes, about 48 per cent of the land in Lower Burma belonged to non-agriculturists, chiefly non-resident, and although the moneylending alien and Indian Chettiar had become the chief holders of such lands, the owners of fields among our friends were also absentee landlords in the fullest sense, having little connection with the working of the paddy, except as a source of income.

Some of the pensioners got a fat income from moneylending although they would not have liked to admit it. Burmans who need money do not borrow from banks, nor do they have dealings with banks as a rule. It is only in this generation that such a thing as a bank balance is becoming common. Borrowing money is always such a shameful thing to Burmans that highly

Father in retirement

usurious rates prevail. The minimum rate of these private money-lenders is Re. 1/8 per Rs. 100/-per month, *i.e.* 18 per cent per annum.

But this emphasis on money-making during the retirement period was not pure avariciousness. It was connected with the ability to discharge the duties of a parent and a good Buddhist during one's last years, to have sufficient means to settle children in a good marriage, which is one of the duties laid down for a good parent, and to make many donations towards pagodas, rest-houses and monasteries, all as a foundation for a rebirth into a better existence.

For men like my father, this last period of their lives was a soft and gentle immersion in the atmosphere which pervaded their childhood in the monastery, and which had been banished into a memory with the years of English education, government posts, courts and litigation, and the rearing of children whose future must be bound up with the obtaining of better government posts.

During these years, my father continued his daily prayers before the altar, but they were short and he said them softly, his feet were shod with shoes and socks, his tourings took him to headmen's houses more often than to monasteries, his evenings were spent in playing tennis instead of chinlon, and drinking lime-juice instead of coconut water, and his houses of the regulation pattern were filled with cane furniture made by convicts in jails. What a far cry from the dim light on wooden floors and pillars, the steady chorus of young monks at prayers. My father, who during his working years had encouraged us to eat, laugh and be merry in each present moment, now dismayed us with a sudden conviction of the vanity of all worldly things, towns, society, dress and ornament. We woke up at dawn to the sound of his prayers, and on most mornings he walked out of the town to the hills where the monasteries and rest houses were gathered; he walked barefoot again with great enjoyment in those quiet grounds, turned aside to supervise the building of a *thein*, a house for the ordination and meditation of monks, which he had persuaded a more wealthy friend to endow. He no longer showered on us de luxe editions of Western encyclopedias and the collected works of Dickens and Scott as he used to, but bought richly carved bookcases and sacred books for the monasteries in Thaton. We no longer ate our meals on chairs, sitting up at a table, but at a low round table on the polished floor. My father sat cross-legged, but he could not go back to eating with his fingers, he still used a spoon and fork.

At nights we fell asleep to the sound of his prayers and it was like a benediction. Buddhist prayers in Burma consist of two parts: the first is a long recitation of precepts and lauds, mostly in Pali and not intelligible to the casual ear. The second part, the *hsu-taung,* is the asking for blessings in a formula which asks: "May (my mother) be blessed. May (a married couple) have long life together." My father worked through a list of all his and my mother's relations and connections. Going down in order of seniority he fitted them all into a rhythm and we came to know the place of each in this melodious chant. When we were young we sometimes waited with bated breath for the turn of a relation

who had just quarreled with my parents, but my father never omitted to ask for blessings on him. We loved this part of our parents' prayers. Uncles, first and second cousins whom we did not see for long stretches of time were kept familiar in this way. Relationships were prefixed to each name; births, deaths and marriages were registered, the infant cousins added, the newly-dead aunts omitted, and the new niece-at-law joined in a long and happy life to her husband. We loved especially our own place in the litany—my sisters, because they were given their full and correct names by which they were never called, and I, because I was an exception, called even in this formal litany by the affectionate name my parents had for me. *"Tha Maung Sett Khaing,"* my father would chant, *"Tha Maung Sett Khaing, Tha-mi Mamie, Tha-mi Ma Mya Thin, Tha-mi Ma Hin Aye, Tha-mi Ma Myat Kyi:* Son Succeeding and Lasting, Daughter Mamie, Daughter Fragrant Emerald, Daughter Cool as the Dew, Daughter Noble and Clear."

Most of the pensioners lived a similar life to my father's at this time. It was indicative of the contentment of their retired existence that they never talked about the business of their past working days when they met. Sometimes they showed a fleeting interest in news of the postings of friends still in service, but even the official matters of Thaton district itself did not enter into their discussions. They talked of charity donations, of the respective monasteries which they endowed and attended, and of formulae of *eggaya-hto,* alchemy, or the search for the philosopher's stone which will turn all metals to gold. Most Burmans get interested in eggaya-hto during their later years, even if few now practice it.

This alchemy, which has no place among the true teachings of Buddhism, has to be done under auspicious astrological influences and is usually carried on in secret. Burman Buddhists condemn the use of it when it is carried on for *lawba,* greed for riches, but others justify the process as a means of concentrating the mental faculties. The common stories tell of hermits in the forests, who by their ascetic life and concentrated meditation have more powers over the forces of nature, as being well versed in the processes of alchemy. When such a hermit achieves the extreme concentration of mind on his task he is successful—the philosopher's stone is discovered, the body of the hermit then disappears in the dissolving of matter, and his spirit is free to live unhampered by the body, till the arrival of the next Buddha on the earth. Most Burmese women, however, although they believe that this happens in the case of hermits, object very strongly to the practice of alchemy on the part of their menfolk, owing to the money and energy that is wasted on seeking out new and expensive formulae once the craze has got hold of a man. All experiments are started with mercury, which is melted with other minerals, animal or vegetable substances which derive their magical properties partly from their inaccessibility, partly from being treated with prescribed rites. My father had no intention of taking up alchemy and impoverishing us, but he too was very interested to hear of the success and failure of various methods. These discussions must have been kept well anchored to reality by the other chief topic of discussion—the families of the pensioners.

The five duties of a parent towards his children include the settling of the child in a good marriage. By the time the a-so-ya mins retire, their sons and daughters have reached a marriageable age. The sons are in the process of winning a good position in one of the government services and their daughters have been dressed with an adequate amount of jewellery. The marriage market, which had no existence in former Burmese society and which still is unheard of in Ye, and among the poorer people, is now a very concrete institution among the educated and modern classes. The rise of the minkadaw class and of higher paid Class I government officials has been mainly responsible for this. More and more within recent years, the higher government services have come to be associated not only with "face," but with *gon*, prestige, and *ausa*, authority, which together make up a *myet-hna-gyi*, big face, in Burma. Mothers of daughters want their daughters to have gon and ausa and be big of face as the wife of the senior government officer in a town, and mothers of sons want to get the most for themselves and their other children out of having such a golden goose. They want a girl with wealth, a meek nature, good looks, religious piety and education, more or less in this order. So that the imperfect daughter-in-law may lack the last named qualities rather than the first. Wealth means not merely money, property or jewels, but an absence of younger brothers and sisters or other potential dependents, this being a very important factor in our closely-knit family system. A relative of mine who had just seen his son enter a top service showed my father his comprehensive table of the marriageable girls of Burma, under headings of family connections, amount and form of property, potential dependents, physical and moral qualities of the girl. My father should have been keenly interested as the father of a son who was studying in England with success, and, indeed, when my brother returned, he might have fetched us about Rs. 30,000 had he desired, so far have we progressed beyond the Burmese traditions of the man's family asking for the hand of the girl with presents of money and jewellery.

It may be asked, what of the men who are thus bartered? Burmans are very greatly attached to their mothers; few can resist a mother's tears, and the tears in these cases are genuinely of grief, because the mother sees this marriage as a faithful discharge of one of her five duties. The five duties of a child towards its parent, on the other hand, include the support of father and mother, and in making this marriage the man sees the best way of providing comfort to his parents in their old age. For the girls also, an arranged marriage is not necessarily a joyless thing. Girls who are educated as we have been, in spite of reading Western romances, are brought up to believe that a girl will grow to love her husband who is good to her. *Tha-na,* pity, compassion, and *chit,* affection-love, are very close in Burmese; the usual way for a wife to address her husband is *Maung,* the same word as younger brother, or *Ko Ko,* elder brother; some husbands address their wives as *nyi-ma-lay*, little sister. And, in fact, in most cases the results do bear out the wisdom of this attitude towards marriage; so that to most Burmans it is the "free" Western marriages which so often appear ill-assorted and lead to divorces. Still, it cannot be denied that much undignified haggling and maneuvering go on nowadays, in the efforts to obtain the best match for sons and daughters. *Aung-thwès,* go-betweens, get a lot of face from bringing something off, money is paid in advance, rush tactics are employed to prevent the man returning from abroad from marrying the sweetheart of his college days, and in some cases even magic is resorted to, though in secret. This black magic, especially, involves some very undignified actions. A younger cousin of mine once warned his mother: "Please, Mother, never try to sell me like a bullock, or worse still to arrange a marriage for my sister. I will not help you to jump thrice on eggshells or throw ten viss of fish into a well at dead of night under instructions from a soothsayer."

Although marriages were constantly being arranged among our circle of friends in Thaton, I was not allowed to attend weddings as a young unmarried girl. What we did attend regularly with the grown-ups were the *u-bok-nay,* the duty day gatherings every week in the rest houses among the hills. On these days Buddhists who choose to observe the day obey eight or ten precepts instead of five. Among these ten are abstaining from food after midday and absence of ornament. In Thaton the observance of this day was made the weekly social event with the same combination of material enjoyment and religious piety that characterizes all Burmese functions as described previously. Each family went to the hills early in the morning with mats, betel boxes and a well-cooked meal. The girls wore all the jewellery they had because we had not yet taken the precepts, and this was a good chance of showing that a family did not lack wealth. We met in the rest houses, to one of which a monk came to intone the precepts. These we repeated in chorus after him; then the elders talked and chewed betel, and at about 10:30 the whole party went to bathe in the pools made by the waterfalls down the hills. We went back to find the pooled dishes of four or five families laid out in a rich feast. We stuffed ourselves with this. The law states that food should not be eaten after noon, and the law was always obeyed in the letter if not in the spirit.

One maiden lady in Rangoon who kept duty days regularly ate till as near noon as she possibly could. She usually finished her meal with fruit, and if she was eating a banana when noon struck with a loud bang from the cannon at the Shwe Dagon Pagoda, "Haw!" she would exclaim, and in would go the whole length of the banana into her mouth. After noon, tea and coffee are not allowed either but aerated waters, which look so much like water, are sanctioned. When my husband was a novice monk in the monastery, they were allowed medicinal products also after noon, and the hungry young novices often made a delicious soup of garlic (a digestive) fried in butter (medicinal component), and water poured on to the fragrant compound.

The younger children of the families also took the precepts, but it was not considered wrong if they felt too hungry or faint to keep to them. Everyone packed up and went home from the rest house at about four in the afternoon. I found these duty evenings very long and depressing. There was no dinner, my father and mother told beads all evening, and at night their mattresses were removed and they slept only on mats.

We were now living in Grandfather's old house. Grandfather had left it to the four youngest among his children, and my mother had bought out the shares of the others because she was sentimentally attached to it and could not bear to see it pulled down. To others it had seemed an unwieldy shape, taking so much good teak which could have built a compact modern house. My mother set about the task of transforming in into a comfortable domestic family house with a nicely disposed front and back, but it was a difficult task. There was no neat garden plot, no face, no bedrooms, but long stretches of gallery and verandah. We fenced off the well so that the village could continue to use it without infringing our privacy, the old big kitchen was dismantled and a compact kitchen made of one of the store-rooms near the washing platform, the old maternity room was stocked with commodes and made into a lavatory, the powder room was used as box-room. Six of us shared the big bedrooms. The altar, the water-pots and meals continued where they had always been. There was a large expanse of shining floor for visitors to sit on mats, and the head of the long verandah held a few chairs. The stable was cleaned up and given to Apana, now an old and rheumy-eyed man, and the downstairs hall, where a school had been, now held our stocks of rubber.

But still there was always so much space, the house seemed vast and empty, and the life so different from our district government houses with a crowd of servants, young men and dependents of all kinds. We felt the change acutely. My sisters were still children who played with each other and had plenty to eat

during their short holidays, but I found the evenings silent and sad with the lifeless echoes which the dim light of the floorboards used to send up. I had been to stay at the house for short periods before my Grandfather died, when I was about three or four years old. Here, where we washed our faces, we looked across to a house now mysteriously barred with a blank wooden face, but then inhabited by *ta-yok chi-thay-mas*, tiny-footed Chinawomen, fabulous creatures according to my nurses, who, though they were slit-eyed and could curse you in an unknown tongue, could be sent reeling back with one touch of a finger. The ta-yok chi-thay-ma had other macabre qualities also. Her child had a big black patch of hair on its arm because it was the reincarnation of his dead sister. At the death of this previous child, the ta-yok chi-thay-ma had frantically grabbed a piece of charcoal and had smudged the arm of the dying child, saying: "If I get this child back in my next labor, may I know her by this mark." Down below the arum bushes grew close and dark against the fence. They had frightened us, like green snakes that must not be touched, because the leaves made your tongue itch with an intangible and incurable itch although the roots were made into delicious soups. In Grandfather's bedroom was a window looking into the maternity chamber, still padlocked with a lock whose key had been lost nearly twenty years ago, and a patch of light wood nailed over the hole which a robber had made with the point of his damyaung. From the maternity chamber, also, an aunt had thrown a basin of washing water to splash on an uncle sitting below, with whom she had quarreled and whose hpon would be lowered by the ignobility of the woman's labor. For my mother the house must have had sharp memories, but she never spoke of them while there because my father became ill shortly after. This oppressed her spirits, and made her think only with sorrow of her dead mother and father, her brothers and sisters, so many now dead and the rest scattered far and never returning after the death of Grandfather.

chapter 7

Aunt Kyi-Kyi Lon—hairdressing—women's clothes—Burmese food—rice—soup—condiments—vegetables—curry—special dishes—sweets

ONE living force had continued at the old house, however, from the time it was built right to the present day. This was my mother's elder sister, our Kyi-Kyi Lon, the same who had thrown herself on the ground at first beholding the muddy fields of Thaton. She had never been to an English school like my mother and indeed had known no other home but the old house all her life. My Kyi-Kyi (aunt-elder-than-parent) is unmarried. The story of how she remained unmarried is stamped with her character.

My eldest aunt was married and died after bearing three children, and the bereaved husband came back to Grandfather and asked for the hand of another aunt so that the children should not lack a loving mother's care. This aunt also died, and the hardy widower again returned to Grandfather. Grandfather might have been persuaded to give another daughter in marriage but Kyi-Kyi Lon, who was next on the list, stamped her feet and shooed the widower away, regardless of the belief that a man who survives two wives is outlived by his third. She inherited my grandfather's spirit and vitriolic temper, and a very lively tongue. When she was young she was round and sturdy and was therefore called Ma Lon, Miss Round. With years of spinsterhood, roundness disappeared, the sturdiness developed into a masculine toughness and her natural abilities turned to business management; her feet broadened and she could tramp for miles; with her sharp tongue she could make men quail. It was our Kyi-Kyi who looked after our rubber estates for us. My mother stood in awe of her, and it was a beautiful lesson in gentle humanity to watch the sisters together. My mother had two aspects to her nature. She had an all-round ability equal to Kyi-Kyi Lon's, but there was a gentleness which tempered every masculine ability she possessed. This tempering was always imposed above. In my aunt's presence, the lower stratum automatically disappeared, because Kyi-Kyi, who quarreled with everyone else, loved my mother like a child who must be scolded and looked after. She therefore devoted her life to our interests.

My aunt never learned English, and derided the refined tones of English pronunciation. She never made the slightest concession to any foreign tongue. Surrounded by a world in which products and institutions bore English names, she took delight in pronouncing unavoidable terms with the broadest Burmese accent. "Ine-Si-Et", she would say for I.C.S., with a marked emphasis on the last word, which is pronounced with a glottal stop, and thus pronounced means "cracked." After listening to a conversation in English she would seize on what she heard most often, "You know" and "I know." "*Yo no, I no, hnit-yauk no, tha-hko ma-la-naing,*" she would say, punning on the word "know," which in Burmese means to wake up. "You wake, I wake, two awake—the thieves cannot come."

Kyi-Kyi lived an independent life; she had inherited a share of the house, among other things, and she lived there on what was due to her from the management of our property. Between her and one servant maid, the old house was kept spotless. A meal was cooked every day for the monastery, and Kyi-Kyi was on very amiable social terms with the monks and the nuns who lived close by. Everyone in Thaton knew her, the young men admired her for lively wit and the women called her a harridan for it. Between visiting us and business and religious good works and scolding everyone, my Kyi-Kyi spent a busy life.

She was so different from my mother. My mother never smoked or chewed betel, but when Kyi-Kyi came we were treated to watching her roll her cheroots. She had the *hsay,* mixture, in a bowl. It was a compound of chopped tobacco leaves, the stem and pith of the *ohn-nè* (coconut flower), and jaggery or sugar. It was a sticky mixture. The wrapping leaves—the leaves of a tree called the *thanat*—were in a cream cracker biscuit tin. In a small cane sieve-tray she had a number of old *a-si-hkans*, stubs of solid ends, about 1½ to 2 inches long; and on a piece of paper was some boiled rice, for sticking. She rolled the mixture in the leaf, tucked the edges of the narrower end neatly in and stuck them down. She stopped the base with one of the a-si-hkans and stuck the leaf over it. This provided a firm grip for the mouth, and the same a-si-hkan could be used again and again. What we loved best about this was that my aunt never used matches but, even when we were little children, she would hand us a cheroot with which we ran to the kitchen. There the cook would pull out a piece of firewood and hold the gigantic flaming match while we puffed the cheroot alight and brought it back to my aunt.

Kyi-Kyi's daily toilet was another thing we loved to watch, and even when I was grown up I never ceased to admire its simple thoroughness. She has never altered it since she was a young girl forty-five years ago, neither conceding to newer fashions nor omitting any of the vanities as she grew from girlhood into middle age. She came out of her bath with her longyi *yi-sha,* that is, drawn up above her bosom. She then put thanakha on face, neck and shoulders; face powder she condemned as having lead in it, but baby's talcum powder she sprayed on her palms, rubbed them together and patted into her face as the thanakha was drying. Then she moistened a brush the size of a baby toothbrush, and rubbed the thanakha off her eyebrows and lashes and traced her hairline in an exaggerated rectangle to produce what was considered a noble and beautiful forehead, a *mahanahpu.* By this time the thanakha and powder were dry, and uneven patches were rubbed off with a dry brush. Then she opened a little jar—always an empty Tiger Balm bottle—in which was a mixture of oil and blacking. She dipped a special brush into this and drew her eyebrows and the rectangular hairline. She cleaned her lips and ear-studs with water, and then put sandalwood or other ground bark on her arms and legs. Her hair had been dressed before she had her bath, in a *sadone.* This is the coil of hair built up in a cylindrical form around a framework of combs and hairpins, helped out by false tresses. It is the universal hair style for all women after they pass the age of about seventeen, and ladies like my aunt never go anywhere unless their hair is formally dressed in this way.

In modern times, however, the younger women have not only streamlined the sadone, making it thinner and taller, but they have shelved it as a full-dress style, to be worn only on special occasions, while every day they go about with the hair drawn straight back and twisted over a comb at the back of the head.

Although the sadone is worn by both older and younger ladies,
differentiating touches are carried out. Young unmarried girls fix
a *sameik* on the right side of the sadone. This is a short tress, the
head of which is anchored hidden inside the cylinder, but which
comes over the top and leaves its free end to dangle coquettishly
at the side. The modern girls exaggerate the coquetry of the
sameik by using an unoiled dry and slightly wavy tress to offer a
wanton contrast to the smooth severe cylinder. In the absence of
permanent waving, and with the straightness of the Burmese
hair, I admired the enterprise of a Rangoon family who subsi-
dized, with supplies of coconut oil, the Indian gardener next
door, an Oriya coming from a race with wavy raven locks, until
his tresses grew to the requisite length and they bought them
for binding into a sameik. This sameik is discarded after marriage, but in the case of a girl who does not get married early, it
continues in a more restrained form, a *sameik-kwin*, when it is
tucked back into the bottom of the cylinder to form a loop.
Shortly after the age of twenty-five, she discards it altogether
and makes just a sadone like a married woman. Kyi-Kyi's sadone
was broad and low; after she had finished the rest of her toilet
she tied her hair by drawing a thread backwards from her forehead so that stray hairs were tucked into the sadone, and the
same with the upswept hair at the back. She also carried the
Burmese powder puff in her luggage though I never saw her use
it. These, which we also still use as the best means of applying
Max Factor powder, were scraps of old cotton vests, about ten
inches square, which had been soaked and washed in thanakha,
thus avoiding the horrible newness of the unused modern powder
puff.

My aunt's clothes were also aggressively her own. This was
noticeable especially with her going-out clothes, for which she
would never have any imported materials. She declared that imported silks, crêpe-de-chines and the like, could not be washed
and beaten clean like the Burmese silks and cottons. Neither did
they produce suitable colors and designs for elderly spinster

ladies like her—they were either gay and skittish, or of a sober-
ness that depressed without pleasing one. What she loved most
were the *ya-khaing* longyis, silks and cottons woven in Arakan,
in small check patterns, but so stout that you soaked them and
beat them hard before the first wearing, and then washed them
again and again until you had a pliant closely-woven fabric
whose color and freshness lasted a lifetime. One of my sisters,
whom my aunt pressed to wear a ya-khaing longyi in preference
to a crêpe-de-chine piece whose bright butterflies had appealed
to her sixteen-year-old fancy, stated that no doubt if she slept in
the ya-khaing longyi every night for seven years, it would just be
at its best for her to wear when she reached the age of twenty-
five. For more dressy occasions, my aunt wore *zin-mè* silks, the
design of which was reputed to come from Chiengmai in Siam,
and in imitation of which Burmese weavers now produce zin-mè
longyis in dull red and green geometrical designs, like old lacquer colors. Kyi-Kyi sometimes wore *Bangauk* longyis also, said
to come truly from Bangkok, but more often woven in Burma in
imitation of the characteristic twist in the weave. These were
produced in smoky blues, ambers and dull greens so beloved of
elderly Burmese ladies.

Silk weaving is one of the old industries of Burma, but the
yarn is mostly imported, for the rearing of silkworms, like fish-
ing, is a form of taking life. Fortunately, around Prome on the
central Irrawaddy, there live a tribe of hill people called Yabeins
who are animists and may safely cultivate the *po-sa,* worm food
mulberry tree. The silk from here is coarse, but is used for the
weaving of the most elaborately patterned silks called *cheik.*
These valuable pieces are used for wedding skirts and ceremonial
wear. Few people possess more than one cheik skirt; the great
number of spools—a hundred or more—necessary to produce the
intricate patterns in minute waves of blended colors makes the
price vary from Rs. 40/- to Rs. 400/- per piece, a high price compared to the present imported silks. All the weaving is done by
hand looms, rectangular frames about five feet long, holding the

warp threads of four yards in length and 40 to 45 inches in width, operated by girls sitting on high stools, raising the alternate threads by a foot-pedal, and banging the pushboard against the woven threads each time they throw the spool across by pulling on a cord, producing eventually an *ok*, a book, a piece for two skirts folded flat and stiff like a book.

With imported yarns dyed with native vegetable dyes, the weavers at Mandalay, Amarapura, Prome and Shwedaung, Kyangin, Tavoy, Kindat and the Yaw valley produced silks of exquisite pinks, blue-greys, gold and amber, strong reds and purples, dull dirty greens, all from the sunset skies, water-vegetation, birds and trees, never fading: *pan-nu, kho, mi-go, hpet-hpu, may-yan, pasun-hsi, payin, kyet-thway, yay-hnyi, a-sein-bok:* tender flowers, dove, smoke, leaf-bud, marian seed, prawn oil, amber, cock's blood, slime-moss, rotten vegetation. Plain colors, checks, stripes and geometrical designs all cost only Rs. 3/- or Rs. 5/- or, perhaps, Rs. 10/- per piece and could be washed forever. No wonder Kyi-Kyi did not understand why we bought imported silks. She did not understand the desire for novelty, for frivolity of birds, giant flowers or sprouting fruit such as are never seen on land or sea.

If my aunt's character and speech were full of sharpnesses with which she jabbed at people, they will all be forgiven her for the sensuous delights which she provided for one and all with her qualities as a cook and an expert on foods. She was such a wonderful cook, she used to be asked to supervise at *a-hlus,* the mass cooking for free feasting of clergy and townspeople. She regarded the feasting of others as her one indulgence in life. In all other respects she economized and denied her tastes like all Burmese spinster ladies, but in the matter of food she considered that we did not live lavishly or plenteously enough. She knew the rarest tit-bits, the physiological effects of eating any particular food, the properties of leaves, the times of year when the most ordinary foods had the greatest beneficent influence.

The field of Burmese food is a rich territory, and so little explored by foreigners, who will normally hear only of the ngapi, rice and salad leaves of the poorest people, that I am tempted to write a whole chapter on it, as dedication to my Kyi-Kyi Lon. The composition of the average plain Burmese meal is: boiled white rice; the *hingyo* or soup; the ngapi or condiment dish; the *to-sa-ya,* "dipper," or raw green vegetable dish which may be classed as a naked salad; the dressed or cooked vegetable dish; and the *hin,* the "curry" of meat or fish to provide the gravy. Roughly, the importance and quantity of each dish are as shown in the diagram.

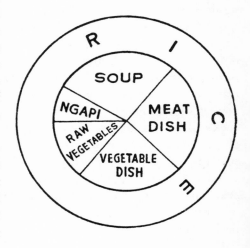

If any visitors are expected there may be one or two other dishes, but this is the standard meal and is enjoyed by all classes of people except the poorest; a-so-ya mins, rich men, clerks and petty traders all eat the same, more or less. For a family of four or five persons two such meals can be provided daily at a cost of about Re. 1/- or Re. 1/4 in an average district town or village. This is for the fresh bazaar, most families storing rice, salt fish and ngapi, and sesamum oil for cooking, by the month or longer periods.

The rice is cooked to result in clean and separate grains. The usual method is to put it on the fire with cold water, using judgment as to the amount of grain and water for the pot. A person who cannot "cut his coat according to his cloth" is *"ko-oh hnin ko hsan ma-tan bè:* his grain and pot do not accord." When, after coming to the boil, the rice is cooked but not yet soft, it is drained by decanting; the water is kept aside for starching the jackets of the women in the daily wash, and the pot is put back on to coals or half off a fire, with the lid left open to let the steam escape and complete the cooking of the rice. It is shaken once or twice during this process, but there is no harm done if a bad servant forgets to do this or puts the pot back on a strong fire, for then the burnt rice is scraped up in a cake (*gyo*) and is eaten, dipped in oil and salt, by the children with great relish.

The soup is always clear. The great majority of soups are plain hingyos, with a stock of fish, prawn or dried prawn, flavored with ngapi, beaten garlic or onion. It is made fresh for each soup, and when it comes to the boil, green vegetables are thrown in and left just long enough to wear down the tough cellulose. The vegetables are never overcooked. Throwing in the vegetables is called *hingyo hkut-tè*, ladling out the soup, and the green things for ladling are numerous indeed. Of leaves, the tamarind, the sorrel, the drumstick (*moringa pterygosperma*), the *kinmun*, the calabash, the mustard, various types of spinach, are only some. Some particular leaves, stalks or fruits require adaptations in the soup they ladle; for example, green chillies with the sorrel, pepper corns with the calabash; and the neem and *mezali* leaves are so bitter that they must be rubbed in salt and cooked three times before they can be eaten. All leaves used for soup have a distinct and delicate flavor. If the soup were strained after the leaves had been boiled in it a few minutes, one could still identify the taste. Richer soups are made with stock of meat— pig's trotters, chicken or duck—and are ladled with dried mushrooms, dried flowers or vermicelli strands, transparent and fair as the lotus.

The ngapi, condiment, dish has several standard forms. "Ngapi" is the general term applied to any of its forms. Usually it comes to the housewife as seinsa ngapi, from Tenasserim, such as is made by my aunts in Ye, or from Yandoon in the Delta region. This high-smelling, strongly flavored paste is stored in glazed earthen jars and flavors almost all dishes or is cooked into its own palatable forms. It is fried with chillies and pounded dried prawns into a crisp brownness, in which form Europeans like it as a toast spread which they call *balachaung*. It tastes something like the product known as Patum Peperium or Gentleman's Relish. More Burmese is *ngapi-chet* (ngapi cooked), when it is fried in a more oily and moist form with tomatoes, tamarind water, green chillies, red chillies, garlic and onion; or *ngapi-daung* (ngapi pounded), when it is pounded into a smooth paste with prawns, ginger, onion and chilly; or *ngapi-thok* (ngapi mixed), when it is made into a salad by baking it dry and then mixing chopped onion, green chillies and citron leaves and a squeeze of lemon.

The to-sa-ya, dipper dish, to dip into the ngapi, of raw green vegetables, consists of leaves, flowers, buds, stalks, and young fruit of all kinds—green mangoes when they are the size of marbles, mango flowers, green marians, *da-nyin-thi*, citron leaves, coriander leaves, cucumbers, *zaung-ya-thi*, *chep-paung-thi*, and a host of others which can be plucked by villagers from hedges or gardens or jungle patches. The dressed vegetables dish may be a *lethok* or a *thanat*. Lethok, hand-wiping-or-mixing, is a mixture of finely shredded or cut vegetable (say green papaya, grown green mango, marian or citron) with the balancing ingredients of oil for mixing smoothly; dried prawn powder and bean powder for filling; tamarind water for sourness if the fruit is not sour; ngapi or fish sauce for salting; green or powdered red chilly for spicing; and crisp fried garlic and onion to set off and dress the whole. In a thanat we can make the orthodox cauliflower, cabbage, brinjals, beans, etc., into a delicious dish by boiling them with vinegar and water till they are not quite cooked, draining them, rolling them in cooked oil in which salt and a little baked ngapi have been dissolved, scattering sesame seeds and crisp fried garlic and onion.

Some vegetables which have a natural succulence are made into thanat uncooked. They are cut up, soaked in vinegar for some hours, drained well and dressed in the same way. Cucum-

ber and horse-radish treated thus are delicious and crunchy. Besides being made into salads, vegetables are "fried." This is not
fat frying. Only the seasoning, consisting of a small quantity of
chopped pork or shrimps, crushed garlic and ngapi, is fried in
the merest fraction of sesamum oil, then the bean sprouts, cabbage or what not, chopped small, are spread over it. This is called
ok-tè, covering with the vegetable; the lid is put on and the
vegetable cooks in the steam from its own water content. Just
before taking it off the fire, it is stirred with soya sauce, and, if
taken off the fire at the correct moment, cauliflower, cabbage,
beans and beansprouts are delicious. Some vegetables lend themselves to an extension of this method in the *kyaw-gyet,* fry-cook,
wnat the English Domestic Science schools call a "combination
method" of cooking. Here the fried seasoning ingredients are
stronger flavored, water is added after the vegetable, and a dish
which is half soup, half curry is produced. Gourds are often
cooked in this way.

The "curry" is called curry for want of a better word. The
Burmese hin does not contain the spices usually associated with
hot curries. The standard hin is the *hsi-byan,* oil-returns-curry,
in which the seasoning and gravy are produced by pounded
chilly, ginger, garlic and onion, fried in oil which has first been
cooked free of moisture. This is fried brown while the meat is
diced and rolled in salt and a little turmeric. Then the meat is
put in and cooked till all its moisture has gone and the "oil returns." Then small quantities of water are added and the pot left
until the meat is tender. The chief meats used are pork, chicken
and duck. Beef and mutton are not liked generally, and many
families, who wish to deny themselves the eating of the flesh of
one animal in order to gain merit, give up beef. The curry described here is only the stock recipe.

There are numerous special meat dishes, steamed, roasted,
sautéd. But it is fish and prawn that Burmese people love best.
We have a great variety of sea and freshwater fish, each lending

itself to special forms of cooking, from the richest nga-tha-lauk, through *nga-myin, nga-gyin, nga-ponna, nga-the-lè-do,* to the black and cheap *nga-gyi* and *nga-khu.* Crabs and crayfish with the lovely red oil in their heads; nga-myin cooked with ginger and soya sauce to make a "sweet" dish or with tamarind and ground chilly to make a peppery one; *nga-hpa-ma* cooked with vinegar and citronella grasses and green chillies into a thick soup, or *nga-yan,* cooked with tamarind water and vegetables into a minestrone; nga-tha-lauk baked so that the flesh is rich and full, but the numerous bones made so soft that they are no longer dangerous to swallow, or nga-khu fried so crisp as to give only a crunch and no taste; nga-ponna cooked into a hsi-byan curry with coriander leaves on top of the fishes, or *nga-bat* cooked and stirred into a flaked consistency; *nga-pè* whose white flesh is kneaded with salt into a glutinous slab to fry in slices, or nga-gyin wrapped in banana leaves with strong flavoring ingredients and steamed in packets until it is ready to melt in your mouth. In their daily meals Burmese people relish the odd parts of animals rather than their flesh—the liver and crop of chickens and ducks, the trotters of pigs, the guts of goats, the entrails of freshwater and, indeed, the heads, tails, fins and roe of all fish.

Besides providing us with rich daily meals, my aunt found great delight in buying vast quantities of foods which were seasonal or only to be bought in certain areas. Mushrooms appearing about May were bought literally in basketfuls, each basket being fifteen inches wide and fifteen high. These were cooked in various ways and eaten by family and servants for about three days on end or longer, until someone suffered from the accumulated toxic effects. Kyi-Kyi also spent days in extracting the red oil from the heads of about fifty crayfish or big prawns. This red stuff gives the flavoring to prawns and we therefore find prawn curries tasteless where the cooks discard the oil with the teeth and other excretions from the heads. Kyi-Kyi filled jars with the rich oil and we kept it through weeks, mixing it with rice and salt. Or she bought about two hundred sparrows at one go and stripped and cooked them unaided. It does not sound sporting to eat sparrows, but the meat of other bigger and more "game" birds is too strong for us. Sparrows when fried crisp are edible to the last shred of bone, little round head and all. It was one of our favorite foods during visits to Thaton, until after my littlest sister got measles and had her head shaved according to custom; when she went about looking so pathetically like the naked birds in the dish that none of us, from my father downwards, could bear to eat a sparrow for a long time afterwards.

All the dishes mentioned above are eaten with rice at the two main meals of the day, but there are also noodle dishes, both wheat and rice noodles, coconut-flavored dishes and others which are eaten at luncheon parties or at mass gatherings of town and village people. At all social functions, also, there is an accompaniment to the cheroots and the betel box in the form of pickled tea-leaf and shredded pickled ginger served in small lacquer trays with nuts, sesamum, prawn powder, fried coconut and garlic. These are all foods eaten at regular times of the day, and as such can be called *sa-sa-ya* foods. But we have not yet ventured into the realm of sweet things, for after a meal only fruit is eaten. All sweet dishes are kept to be eaten *between* meals, and as such are called *tha-yay-sa*, food for the saliva, and only incidentally for nourishment.

Tha-yay-sa usually means something sweet because there are so many sweet ones, but what does produce more saliva than any other are the sour ones. A favorite Burmese afternoon pastime is the eating of sour and green fruit with ngapi and chilly, in order to offset the drowsiness of the heat. Green mangoes, marians, chep-paung-thi, *yay-ngan-thi,* gwe-thi, *thit-to-thi* range through all degrees of sourness till you come to *ton-kyin-thi,* shiver-sour-fruit, so sour that you shiver when you bite it. On rainy afternoons we felt too chilly to eat these and nibbled at things with a nutty flavor. Roots, tubers, seeds and nuts are eaten dipped in raw sesamum oil and salt—the roots of the palmyra, and of a bean (*pè-myit*), arrowroot and sweet potatoes, chestnuts and the boiled seeds of the jack tree.

But when we come to the real sweetmeats, what richness, what variety is there! As exiles of the Japanese War, we collect in parties to eat uninteresting and foreign foods, but after the meal we gather round and add flavor to the whole evening as we list all the tha-yay-sa we used to eat, some of them not since we were children—and excitement and salivation and comfort in each other's company mount as one after another throws in a fresh contribution to the list, bringing back with sharp delight some half-forgotten taste from a childhood paradise. The names of our sweetmeats are all descriptive of something, their appearance, consistency, composition, or associations which they have, so that the mere recitation of them gives one delight. Sweets which are in balls: *mon-pein-nè-si, mon-lon-yay-paw, mon-longyi, kalapè so:* cake jackseeds, cake-balls floating, big cake-ball, cake-wee-gram-balls. Those that are in round wafer shapes: *mon-pyissa-lè, mon-hsi-kyaw, bein-mon, mon-lè-bway:* worthless cake, fried-in-oil cake, wheel cake, whirlwind cake, which can be crushed into a mouthful from a circumference of about fifteen inches. Those that come as noodly bits of flour or grain, lathered or drowned in coconut juices: *mon-baing-daung, mon-lok-saung, mon-hsan:* cake in stick pieces, cake made by covering, cake sprinkled. Those rich cakes of flour, nuts and raisins which are cut in diamond shapes from slabs twenty inches in diameter: *hsa-nwin ma-kin, kyauk-chaw, pa-thein halawa, mon-kywè-thè* or *mon-ka-lame:* cake-not-free-from-tumeric, cake-smooth-as-marble, Bassein cake, cake-buffaloes'-liver or cake-black-Indian, so black and glossy is it. Or those that come in shapes of things: *mon-leit-pya, mon-let-kauk, bi-mon, daung-kwa-mon:* cake-butterfly, cake-bangle, comb cake, peacock's hoof cake. These sweets range through all consistencies from compressed cake form to almost liquid jelly; their ingredients are from sources as widely apart as the fruit of the palmyra and the groundnut. Most of them are freshly made, and women

and men sellers walk around with them during the hours between breakfast and dinner, from about 11 A.M. to 5 P.M.

Sometimes a child sees a miracle when all these delights are gathered before its eyes and ready only for the asking. This is at a *Neibban Zay*, a Nirvana Bazaar, a paradise on earth to the child. Kyi-Kyi once took me and my small sister to a Neibban Zay when the rest of the family were away. In the absence of my mother's more sophisticated tastes, Kyi-Kyi smeared thanakha all over Pusu's body, dressed her only in a petticoat and wooden slippers so that she should keep as cool as possible and led her by the hand to Nirvana. Three streets of householders were giving a free feast to the town; each house had a stall before it and was serving a different mon from the next. Children wandered up and down, stopping before the sweet they liked best, stuffing themselves to their heart's content, because the Neibban Zay was

being given as a work of merit and grown-ups would not inter-
fere with the distribution of charity. Never shall I forget my
Pusu walking up that street, her neck craned and her eyes round
with wonder and appetite, her thanakha legs sticking out brown
and chalky from under her white petticoat.

Hand in hand with the keen delight in the tastes of food goes
our interest in the physiological effects of foods. Thus medicine
and food are closely allied, and the good health of a normally
constituted person is maintained with very little reliance on bot-
tled tonics, even among modern townspeople. For this reason,
too, Burmese people often eat foods which are not altogether
good for them but the taste of which they like, and they rely on
the counteracting effect of the antidote food which is usually
contained in the recipe. "Neutralization is more epicurean than
prevention." Just as the cooling mangosteen is eaten after the
heating durian, the pickled tea-leaf which contracts the men-
strual flow of women is eaten with ginger, which, shredded and
pickled in lemon juice, can be eaten in large amounts to have a
counteracting effect. Cucumber also causes *lay-hto-tè*, the wind-
to-pierce in the body, but citron is *lay-naing-tè*, conquers wind.
Citron leaves and cucumber are often seen on the same to-sa-ya
plate. Mushrooms, which have a toxic effect, are cooked with the
water-greens called *ga-zun-ywet*, which not only counteract the
poison but also provide a neutralizing green taste to the richness
of mushrooms. When we were constipated, my mother gave us a
sherbet of tamarind, sweetened with jaggery—the cooked sugar
juices of the palmyra palm—both of which are purging. The
sherbet tasted cool and delicious and the jaggery has, in addition, a soothing effect on the stomach and intestinal linings.
Guavas are best eaten green and crisp, when they might give one
a stomach ache, but in any case they taste better when dipped in
yet-sa, the linctus powder with digestive properties. There are
numerous other examples. A crowning one may be seen in the
zi-byu-thi, the Indian gooseberry, which has an astringent taste
that on drinking water leaves a clean sweetness in the mouth.

The contracting effect of this on the menstruation of a woman is considered so great that some elders say: "A girl has but to sit under a zibyu tree for her menstruation to stop." College girls of Rangoon University used to eat these fruits by the pile, sucking the pungent juices out of each bite as they talked and talked, and then they all trooped out to the college food shop, where they each ate one anna's worth of ginger salad and never knew any ill effects.

chapter 8

Vernacular and English schools—the University—position of women students—a student strike—student romance—drama, dancers, and clowns—verbal humor

WE lived at Thaton for two years, and then my father became ill and had to be moved to Rangoon for treatment. This meant the packing up of the household, and when my father died shortly afterwards, my mother never went back to live at the great echoing house, but stayed in Rangoon to be near our schools. Thus the long period of our district life came to an end. From now onwards, my mother and sisters were to become merged in the increasing company of *Yan-gon-thu*, Rangoon dwellers, but we saw nothing of this life yet. School walls and student interests at the University enfolded us, and our holidays were spent at Ye and other country places. I was already at the University by this time, after having spent nine years at an English school—nine years during which the alternating periods of school and holidays transported me by turns into two completely different worlds, each kept shut off from the other by childish self-consciousness and reticence. The educational system in Burma did not have a homogeneous structure owing to the different media of instruction in use, and I have always felt that we were the particular victims of this shortcoming. Mistakenly sent to exclusive schools, we were denied the company of a great crowd of Burmese playmates during the greater part of these nine years.

Classified according to the language of instruction, there were three types of schools in Burma—the Vernacular, the Anglo-Vernacular and the European. There were over 5,000 recognized vernacular schools in Burma, which contributed towards raising the literacy of the poorest classes, but did little more. The pupils could not hope to continue their studies at the University, where the medium of instruction was English, and although high-school classes were introduced after 1931, they did not qualify a student for any post except that of teaching in such a school. There were few well-paid posts open to those without a knowledge of English.

The great bulk of schools in Burma were Anglo-Vernacular schools, where instruction was carried on in Burmese, but English was taught as a subject; and in the highest classes, some of the text-books used were in English, as the translation of schoolbooks into Burmese was still at an infant stage. My experiences of teaching at the Teachers' Training College, Rangoon, where we had an Anglo-Vernacular school for model teaching and practical training of educational students, were a fair example of the multiple forms of instruction prevailing. I taught in Burmese from a text-book which had not yet been translated into Burmese, as the subject, Home Science, was a new one. I explained the lesson and questioned the pupils in Burmese, but when summing up the points on the blackboard, wrote in English, so that the copying children could more easily correlate the matter with the

contents of their English text-books. When answering examinations they were free to write in English or Burmese, and there
were many who had a deficient knowledge of English but preferred to write in this language because the text-book had been
in English. Among the educational students taking notes, also,
there might be included a few Anglo-Burman students who did
not know Burmese well. Up to 1935 it was still possible to enter
Rangoon University without any knowledge of Burmese, and one
grade of the Burmese "lectures" there started with the learning
of the alphabet, progressing to the stage of writing sentences by
the end of the two-year course. Almost all towns with a population of more than 5,000 inhabitants had a girls' school and a
mixed school of the Anglo-Vernacular type—either government
or mission or national schools, which later received government
aid. The majority of the students at the University was from
these Anglo-Vernacular schools.

Finally there were the European Code schools, teaching in
English with Burmese as an alternative second language to
French or even to Additional English in the high school, until
about 1933, when Burmese was made the compulsory second language and the standard of it was also raised to approximate more
closely to the Anglo-Vernacular standard.

When my brother and I were first to be sent to school, about 22
years ago, government officials like my father were still under the
impression that education in an English school would give a child
a great advantage in making his way in Burma. All the examinations for higher government services were conducted in English,
and all well-paid posts required a knowledge of English. We
were therefore sent to a European Code school, although such
schools were started primarily for English-speaking children.
Owing to the peculiar social conditions prevailing in the schools
at the time, we underwent acute misery during all the years that
we were there. Such schools, for both boys and girls, were set up
in the big towns, Rangoon, Mandalay, Moulmein, Maymyo,
Toungoo, etc. Most of them were mission or religious schools,

aided by the government and by the diocese or a religious mission.

Very few Burmans at that time sent daughters to such schools, though sons were sent commonly enough, and the distinctions made against the stray natives who entered the rolls began from the moment of entry. The diocesan schools insisted on our adopting English Christian and surnames, from an aversion to including heathen names on their registers. Burman Buddhist were thus transformed into orthodox Christian names: Sir Htoon Aung Gyaw and his brothers became a family of Thompsons, Sir Paw Tun was happily converted into Potter, and my brother U Sett Khaing, with less relevance, became Robert Downs. Thus many distinguished Burmans spent years under these assumed names. The Roman Catholic schools were kinder. They merely required us to adopt a system of first name and surname, which does not exist among Burmans, and wished us to pick a Christian first name so that the nuns could pronounce it easily. Thus we got Kathleen Maung, Grace Nee, Sarah Tin Gyi, the daughters of U Maung Maung, U Nee and U Tin Gyi. My own name Mi Mi Khaing was brought into line as Mamie Khaing.

We went to a Roman Catholic convent, where the nuns made no attacks on Buddhism and no attempts to proselytize us— despite which I became attracted to their religion for a few years—but with sincere conviction and fervor they condemned everything else in us that was different from the great mass of Anglo-Burmans who filled the school. A good portion of these were the children of Englishmen who, not having entered into a legal marriage with the Burmese mothers, had now left mother and child with a sum of money which the kind nuns stretched to cover as much schooling as was possible. These and other Anglo-Burman children were encouraged to swank over us with childish cruelty about our darker skins, flat noses, and uncurling hair. They did this to such an extent that many of us in our minority and our helpless misery branded our distinguished parents as being "half Burmese and half English," in order to gain their good opinion. We were told that Burmese food was stinking, that the use of oil for the hair was dirty and insanitary, and when young sisters ran after their elder ones calling Ma Ma, Elder Sister, all the children hooted with laughter. No wonder that my sister Mya Mya during her first weeks at school would sit by the gate, evening after evening, singing mournfully:

> *May May yay-ay*
> *La pa taw*
> *Kyi-gan ta-maw maw.*

> Oh mother, mother,
> When will you come?
> The crow is tired with a-cawing.

But conditions improved with time; we grew older and less imaginative, and above all the tide of Burmese nationalist feeling which surged into being in about 1920 was at last beginning to seep through the convent walls.

Even the nuns heard, in 1930, about Saya San, who raised a rebellion in Tharawaddy district, and roused such fervor among a certain section of the population that about 2,000 rebel followers were killed—their bodies vulnerable to gunfire in spite of the charms they had tattooed on—before the Government succeeded in suppressing the rebellion. Although Saya San was a charlatan to those in authority, and his followers a band of unruly dacoits, his conviction that he was born to become the monarch of a newly resurrected Burmese kingdom fired the imagination of some nationalists. To them he was an intrepid spirit, his courage so keen and his body so hardy: *Kya ko Khalok, thitngok hnin hsu ko thinbyu*: The tiger his stubbing stone, tree stumps and bushes of thorns his smoothest mat. By the time the nuns had heard of Saya San I had another Burmese girl as a fellow boarder and classmate. Grace Nee was a girl of great spirit and mental liveliness. Her father was also an a-so-ya min, and we derived great comfort and happiness from each other's presence. When the class-teacher scolded one of us, saying, "You Burmans nowadays are expecting us to kow-tow to you. Yes, this mad fellow Saya San. And you think that we must bow to you," then the other would bang desk and chair in sympathy and indignation. Our hearts would swell to bursting point, for though we knew little yet about nationalism or patriotism, we identified our country and our race with the persons of our parents, and we could hardly bear this constant humiliation of their name. We shrank from telling them about it, however. My father and mother never knew how different our life at school was from the world at home.

What a glorious new world opened out before us when we went to the University. What splendor there was in the richness of Burmese dress, food, companions, religious celebration, music, dancing and wit. I only regret that I could not take full advantage of these years because family troubles tumbled around my ears just then, and when they had subsided I was forced into earnest study to win the best degree possible in order to comfort my mother. This was necessary because up till this time I had always disappointed my parents because I had preferred popularity among companions to concentration on studies. Rangoon University, which was embodied in 1920 from two colleges which had been affiliated to Calcutta University, now consisted of four constituent colleges—University College, Judson College, Teachers' Training College and Medical College. Of these, the Teachers' Training College led a self-sufficient collegiate life of its own, with its normal school, its Anglo-Vernacular high school and its graduate students. Judson College, which was an American missionary college, contained a very large percentage of Karens and Christians. Medical College was situated a good distance away from the University estate, and in any case students did not enter its buildings until their third year. For the great majority of Burman Buddhists, therefore, the University meant University College with its strength of about 200 women and 800 men students.

The buildings of the college were laid out on a garden estate of the University, about four miles out of Rangoon. There were brick and wood residential halls grouped in units, great blocks of teaching buildings in a series of rectangular arms from a main block, a University Convocation Hall in the form of a massive square structure laid heavily at the head of a fine central drive, a narrower and lofty University Library building, a Union Hall, a gymnasium with bright dancing murals on its outside walls, and later a Buddhist Congregational Hall with the traditional tiered roofs in concrete. Opposite was Judson College in the same style, but with the scale greatly contracted. The whole arrangement was set out with stretches of grassy lawns, gardens, great trees and the thousand smaller trees, which had been planted when the estate was first laid, and residential houses for the staff; and bordering all were the Kokine Lakes, extensive stretches of water with pretty banks and wooded islands.

The University estate could have been developed into a self-sufficient garden city for it had already a post office, a bookshop and a small hospital of its own, and a servants' village stretched out till it joined the Teachers' Training College not far away. Although the blocks of modern structures could have been built in a more Burmese style, there was enough romance in these surroundings for those of us who had come from English schools. The Convocation Hall was guarded by two giant bronze gryphons squatting on slabs of concrete, in the way that lion gryphons guard all our pagodas. The names of the residential halls were the names of ancient capitals of Burma—Prome, Tagaung, Pagan and Ava; Pegu, Thaton, Sagaing and Inya. The bus service connecting the University with Rangoon town was marked with the naga—the dragon of our mythology and a noble beneficent creature. It was the most elevated of the Rangoon Electric Tramway's attempts at symbols for the illiterate users of buses—an airplane for Mingaladon, where the airport of Rangoon was situated, a horse's head for the suburb of Insein, where wild horses used to graze before the area was cleared and built up, a prawn for the suburb of Pasundaung, which means "Mountain of Prawns" and a naga for the *Tegatho*, the Taxila of learning.

Burmese girls and boys came to this University from the age of sixteen upwards. They studied English and Burmese and a combination of three other subjects for two years, reducible to one for more promising students, and then took an Intermediate Arts or Science examination. After this, a small percentage read an Honors Course for three years, and the great majority took a B.A. or a B.Sc. with a combination of three subjects. There were facilities for an M.A. course, a Law Degree, and an Engineering Degree in a special Engineering College endowed by the Burma Oil Company. For graduates who wished to return to cram for a competitive examination for one of the government services, there was a useful system of minor tutorship posts which, originally paying Rs. 120/- per month, had been split up into two or three posts paying Rs. 40/- to Rs. 60/- for about four to six hours of work per week. This enabled students to have an extra year or two of preparation without any support from home, because boarding fees in any of the halls amounted to Rs. 24/- only. Indeed for the richer classes of Burmese people, life at the University was one of the cheapest ways of passing years in pleasant surroundings, and only the existing rules prevented some from continuing their adolescence into their late thirties. One of my cousins, who showed such promise that he matriculated at fifteen, became a rowing man with much money to spend after he joined the University and spent altogether fifteen years as an undergraduate, dodging from one college to another, alternating the arts and the sciences as a reason for his long stay. My uncle Kyaw Din, who carried off the prize of the year in his Intermediate examination, subsequently spent seven years getting his B.A. because he was the best footballer of his day.

Although there were students here and there who were buried in books either from a love of learning or from being the only breadwinner of a family, my remembrance of University College, Rangoon, is of a great mass of boys and girls who tried to get a passable degree round examination time, but were otherwise submerged in a flood of love and dramatic entertainment. The various associations of arts and sciences, religious and racial fraternities, were more social than intellectual in their activities, but in the Union there was no lack of exciting and impassioned discussions. Here it was that Thakin Nu, Foreign Minister during the Japanese occupation, and Major-General Aung San, leader of the Burmese National Army, harangued us as junior students. Here there was much fierce heartburning about agrarian troubles, labor strikes at the Yenangyaung oilfields, support of Ministers, and the indifference of the less worthy sections of University staff and students towards the nationalist movement.

The crowning event of my years there was the great strike of 1936, when about 600 students got into buses just before the final examinations and encamped themselves on the slopes of the Shwe Dagon Pagoda hill, with much sympathy and material support from the public, the men returning every morning to picket the black-leg examination candidates by lying across all exits and entrances—a completely successful technique, for it is an unthinkable insult to a Buddhist male to have his body trodden on, and no Burman or Burma Indian, or Chinese for that matter, will dare to inflict such an insult.

Some of the strikers felt, after the rallying speeches in the Union, that they were striking to evict an immoral member of the staff who had the support of the Principal, whom they considered an autocrat; others knew that definite demands had been put forward for the amendment of the University Act, the ultimate result of which would be to make the Principal more accountable to Burmese political leaders; a great majority felt a wave of unnameable exaltation as they stormed hall after hall for recruits, ringing bells and shouting, "Come on, sisters, the day of freedom has arrived at last;" and almost all banged and cheered as they drove away, on the roofs, the steps and the wheels of the buses, at the thought of no examinations that year, and the exciting days of picketing ahead. But it was a tragic and unhappy time for some who did not have money to waste on another year before graduation and who trusted that the authorities would succeed in holding the examinations, or for others who did not join out of personal loyalties of the moment and who had friends and brothers with impassioned convictions on the other side. I shall always remember the face of my friend Ko Ohn as he refused to let a doctor into Inya Hall to attend to a sick non-striker, his good face so full of distress and his longyi all smudged with the melted tarmac of the road in which he had been lying under the hot March sun. "Please, we must do it," he said; "I am so thirsty and my head is aching, but we must do it for our country."

One of the reasons for the focussing of public interest on the University students was the great interest taken in the development of the young women there. The male students, like the public, were not interested in them only for reasons of courtship or companionship, but took a keen objective interest in them. It has been said of Burma that she has no feminist movements because none have been necessary; the women have always had all the rights they wanted. But it goes further than that. Burmese men take a sincere pride in the achievements of a woman who can successfully invade spheres outside her domestic tasks. Far from the medical and legal professions presenting a closed phalanx to the first women seeking to enter, Burmans love to introduce their distinguished women as "the first lady doctor" and "the first lady barrister." On the other hand they demand that on no account shall a woman take on mannish and immodest behavior and outlook with her new abilities. Allowances will be made, if necessary, for weaker constitutions, extra time spent on the making of formal sadone hair style before attending work, or for soft voices.

Hence, in University College, where there was a generation of adolescent girls, some of whom had never before been to Rangoon from their district schools, the greatest interest was taken in their line of development—their scholastic success, their interest in or indifference to politics and nationalism, the degree of their response to Westernizing influences, their clothes and their morals—and yet the most censorious interest was not to be taken as personal or malicious. It was concern for the future of Bur-

mese womanhood, we were told. Thus no woman student had
any private life or anonymity. Whatever characteristics she possessed were taken up by a few who were interested in those particular qualities and then received the attentions of the great body
of men students, who only wanted something to sharpen their wit
on. The height of this interfering concern, on the part of young
men, for the moral welfare of young women was reached in 1940
when a petition was seriously put up to the Principal of University College, by a number of students, that certain young
women be ordered to shorten the shoulder straps of the orna-
mental bodices worn under the transparent jackets. So sincere
was their solicitude that the Principal felt constrained to refer the
matter to the Warden of the Women's Hall for action.

But the young men were not stinting in approval either, even
though the majority expressed it in loud good-natured chaff. In
fact, for a keen interest in politics, for wit, for exquisite coyness
or a proud beauty, the girls in University College were in as
much limelight as can surround a rugger hero at an English University. And indeed, the word "hero" was used for them because
the word "heroine" could not be shouted in Burmese euphony.
Hence, if a report had gone abroad that a girl had swum the
2,000 yards of the cross-lake track, or had harangued a group of
young men for bad manners, or was coming to a lecture with her
hair in an informal knot at the back of her head instead of a
formal sadone, she was greeted on entrance by a hundred odd
youths stamping and cheering and jeering and all shouting,
"Hero! Hero!"

No wonder there was love everywhere. Even in modern Rangoon an unmarried young man and woman could not be seen
without the presence of a third person, but sentimental love
flourished all the more for that. It surged up among all the back
benches of the lecture rooms and flowed into the corridors where
the poor stricken couples blushed and spoke in whispers in spite
of the applause of all passers-by. It flowed along the shores of the
Inya Lake, on whose banks the girls walked in groups of two or

three after their evening bath and toilet, and the youths walked in other bands until they met and spoke to the girls. Particularly on the fine evenings of the first monsoon or the first cool dry weather after the deluge had spent itself, the shores of Inya Lake presented a scene of the greatest human felicity. All that was sweet in life seemed to be collected there—youth and pretty faces, fine Burmese silks and newly washed hair, anticipations of joyful meetings, the clear calm water and the brilliant evening sky, the islands in the distance and the bands of young men singing sad songs by the water's edge.

Dramatic entertainment was very rich at the University. It was rarely that the students themselves performed in musical concerts or stage dancing, but troupes of actors were hired to give performances at all celebrations of sports victories, scholastic successes, farewells to popular tutors who had got into government service, or celebrations of religious festivals. The traditional Burmese stage-play is the *zat-pwè*, the staging of one of a few well-known stories, based mainly on the Jatakas, which are stories showing incarnations of the Buddha in his various existences on this earth. Such were the *Wethandaya Zat*, the *Mahaw Zat*, of U Kyn U, the stories of Buddha's life as Prince Wethandaya and as Mahaw, son of a rich nobleman. Written in this form all zats, whether based on the Jatakas or not, contained episodes to provide King and Minister scenes, doleful partings and the weeping dirge of the heroine, scenes of clowning, or sorcerers and heavenly spirits and, highlight of all, the happy meeting scene of the Prince-Hero and the Princess-Heroine, when they sing and dance and joke with the attendant characters, singly and together, for a whole hour or two maybe, while they and the audience forget the thread of the story in the wonderful agile dancing of the hero, his feet falling as softly and as lightly as a kitten's paws but with all the speed, the unexpected turns, the beauty of body and of costume, which make the male zat dancer the essence of the national gaiety. In our time, the old zat plays are treated much as the miracle plays of Elizabethan England probably were—the plot is there, but each company of actors uses the play to hold its own songs, dances and comic lines. The zat lasts for hours, all the night through until sunrise, but the form of it is such that the audience sees it as episodes against a known background of plot, and can thus eat, talk or even doze during the tedious connecting scenes and sit up in enthralled silence for the first appearance of the hero, the duet dances, the songs of the heroine.

We could not stage these shows at the University owing to the length of them and the difficulty of procuring a company. We saw them often in childhood when there were two great companies touring the districts. Po Sein and Sein Gadon came with their companies to the district towns; they hired the local hall, and then charged their audiences by mat-space. Buyers of spaces came earlier in the day and laid down their thinbyus over the rough bamboo mats provided. At night the whole family, including grandmothers and young children, arrived with pillows, fans, goblets of drinking water and things to eat, and squatted and reclined each on its own mat. Vendors of pickled tea and jujube plums, both of which have the effect of keeping one awake, walked in and sold their packets without a license, but just as an overflow from the row of food stalls that had sprung up in the lane leading to the hall.

At the University, however, we always staged *anyein-pwès*, and not these night-long zat-pwès. An anyein is a much handier, more compact sort of entertainment. The troupe consists of two clowns, one chief dancing girl and two subsidiary ones, and a band of musicians. Such a troupe can be hired for about Rs. 40/-. No seats are ever bought for an anyein; people hire them to celebrate weddings, shinbyus and other happy events. They perform on a rough open-air stage, and the show is free to all who wish to flock to see it. The poorest beggars may perch themselves on neighbʼring trees and fences to enjoy the four- or five-hour program of songs, dances and jokes.

When an anyein was held at University College, we entered the grounds at about 7 P.M. and found the stage with its rear occupied by the orchestra tuning instruments and practicing snatches of the airs; in the center a basinful of offerings to propitiate the nat-spirits so that the entertainment will be a success; and at the opposite corners of the front of the stage the two clowns squatting, watching the audience enter and uttering declamations about the occasion of the entertainment; but as yet in a very desultory fashion, while they scratched their heads, cleaned their ears and chewed betel, because nobody was ready to pay full attention. Very shortly, however, the orchestra came to life in a harmonious concert. Within the circular frames of two big harmonicums, about two to three feet high and four to five feet in diameter, sat the master players. The kyi-waing master was surrounded by a row of graduated gongs strung along the inside of the harmonicum, which he struck with a knobbed stick in quick melody. The *saing-waing* master produced a thinner strain from his graduated drums, which he struck with the flat of his fingers. Between the two sat a *hnè* player, blowing loudly his oboe, which had a wide bell-shaped mouth; the *pulway* master played lively dancing notes on his flute; a gentle looking youth kept rhythm with a pair of brass cymbals; and an energetic youngster banged his split bamboo clapper in the same syncopation. At intervals could be heard the patala player, who struck melodiously with two bamboo sticks on thin slats of bamboo laid side by side on the strings of a long narrow box which dipped in the center and ascended at the ends.

While the orchestra thus practiced and played and the clowns talked half-heartedly and the people streamed in, one of the subsidiary dancing girls was carrying out her toilet at the left rear of the stage, with a mirror propped against a box and in full view of the audience. The dancer's dress is an adaptation of the formal Burmese court dress, the adaptations being in the direction of making it more coquettish and frivolous. The basque of the tight-fighting silk jacket is stiffened with bamboo wire in the seams and hems to make it curve up like wings from waist and hips; the unseamed skirt, which is folded over tightly and pinned down on one side with only a knee-high slit to allow dancing movements, is held in place by a belt with a big ornate buckle, whereas a woman of dignified movements should be able to keep her longyi up with only a deft twist—hence the expression *"htamein ma-naing, pawa ma-naing:* no mastery of skirt, no mastery of scarf" as a description of a slovenly woman; the hair is in a cylindrical woman's sadone with a floating side-tress, but part of it also hangs down in a fringe all around after the fashion of a girl in her early teens, and the whole cylinder is covered with sprigs of flowers; the face is painted chalk white by the addition of a cosmetic containing lead to the thanakha, the favorite brand being called in Burmese *"B Nga Lon: Five B's"*, with the parenthetic explanation in English: "Burma Brand Burmese Belle's Beautifier;" a gauzy scarf and a fan set off the young dancing lady, but, unfortunately, her small and lively feet are encased in white cotton socks in order to provide a whiter effect than the Five B's can do.

By the time her toilet is done, the audience is already seated, the clowns are getting bored and begin to shout for her with mock honorifics. The dancer comes out with a wooden face and lackadaisical air, makes obeisance to the audience and to the basinful of offerings, and then sits with her knees tucked under her, presenting to the crowd a winged back of perfect indifference. The clowns now launch into a description of her person, talents and reputation with mock rhapsodies and many bawdy puns. Then they formally call on her to dance and, just as the audience begins to grow a bit restive, the girl rises, turns around and gives one quick short dance. From now on the program can go ahead with a swing. Jokes, antics, songs, dances and repartee follow in fast succession, with the orchestra accompanying. After an hour the next girl takes the stage, followed at about 10 P.M by the chief dancer, according to the universal rule in Burmese entertainment that the best bit is worth waiting for and must be reserved to the last.

All this while, the dancing girl—the *minthami*—is a most de-

lightful creature, fascinating by the combination of wanton behavior with the still and formal dress which makes a flat and
angular doll of her, being open to the most lewd jokes by the
clowns while she protests a chaste morality in reply to their
quips. She hits the clowns with her fan, claps her hands and
stamps her feet, plays with her scarf and rearranges her dress
with great care, disregarding the audience altogether, asks for a
cigarette or a drink of water when she wants it, gets a Burmese
powder puff passed to her after an energetic dance and gets the
clowns to fan her with mock earnestness and many jokes about
her sweating, lets her eye rove among the audience until it has
lighted on the football or rowing hero of the hour, and gets teased
with him throughout the evening. These dancing girls considered
it a feather in their cap to be known as a favorite of the University students, and many of them adopted titles conferred on
them for successful performances at the colleges. Academic titles
were invested with glamor through being in Pali or in English—
Weiksa Mè, Unibarsity Mya Than Kyi, Tegatho Thein Tin, Col-

leik Sein: Graduate Damsel, University Mya Than Kyi, Taxtila Thein Tin and College Sein, a zat dancer of more status.

The jokes of the clowns were mostly based on pornographic punning, in their sallies with the dancer, in descriptions of current events such as elections, pagoda festivals, the football match which has just been won, or an Indian film which is being advertised, and on mispronunciation of English words to give them a bawdy meaning. In fact, they were amusing in the way of good music hall gags, but in an anyein the clowns needed more native wit and quickness, for not only did they extemporize by quips at the audience, exercising their fancy at a dog that howled or a foreigner sitting in the back rows, but the audience itself was free to join in and challenge their sharpness.

The songs sung, however, were not vulgar songs; they were pretty or serious and were mostly written specially in honor of the occasion. No matter what the reason for the staging of the anyein, the song-writers did not find accurate description an impediment to their poetic fancy, fitting details of the time, place and sponsors to rhyme and rhythm. When an Anglo-Burman student and I won State scholarships in 1937, Inya Hall, the residential hall for women, held an anyein, and the song of the evening had a refrain which repeated: *"Mi Mi yè, Kathleen yè, Ahkya-bwè:* Oh Mi Mi, Oh Kathleen, how much to be admired and emulated!" Unfortunately, by the time I returned home the tune had been fitted to more popular words and I never learned the original version, but I do remember the song written as an accompaniment for the dance of Ma Ohn, a talented student from Mandalay, who took part as representative performer of the University in an entertainment given for the funds of the National Girls' School. The words show the characteristic happy mixture of song and description:

> *Yatanadon Man Shwe Myo thu,*
> *Thabaw kaung hnin say-da-na hpyu*
> *Varsity nan myi yu*

Kyaung-gyi colleik thu.
A-hok ko bin thabaw tu,
Ta-gè ko bin manaw hpyu
Myoma kyaung a-hlu
Waing wun ka-pa-ku.
Yandon ngway ko say-da-na hta ya
Way-bya myat kyi hpyu
Amyo thami Boddha ba-tha
Taing ee ee sa hpyu
Aung lan ta lu lu
Nameik kaung thabaw hmat yu,
Myoma kyaung a twet—hsaung ywet lo ku
　　　　　　　　hsaung ywet lo ku
Pyo pyo Ohn ko Shwe Daing Nyun ga thachin
　　　yay pay tè thu.

Dweller of Mandalay, City of Jewels,
With a generous heart
To come and take part
As student of our greatest schools.
Indeed so willing
So glad to be filling
Our need for the cause of the National School.
With mind so kind towards the fund
For Buddhist girls, our country's dower,
As this succeeds our plans shall flower.
She comes to dance for the National School,
She comes to dance,
She comes to dance,
Young lady Ohn, sweet, single, pretty,
For whom Shwe Daing Nyun has written this ditty.

We laughed loud and long at the jokes of our most popular pair
of clowns—a thin shrivelled man called Hnyat-Gyi ("great nut-
cracker") and a big well-fed man called Dambouk ("pillau
rice")—on the occasions when we could hear them, but during
the intervals our daily companions at the University did not
allow us to miss them very much. The average Burman spends

158

puns and jokes

much time and thought, comparatively speaking, on making puns and spoonerisms, fashioning riddles and conceits to spice or flower his normal speech, and both the native wit and the monosyllabic language ensure a roaring success. It was the commonest thing to pass a crowd of students sitting or standing around having a verbal contest, and to hear at intervals a cheering and clapping as they shouted "Point! Point!," which English word they had adopted for applauding a telling thrust. This interest in wit enabled our lecturers to enliven their discourses with spontaneous humor rather than to draw upon a perennial stock of jokes. There were both serious and frivolous uses of this privilege. We had two serious old Burmese lecturers—Saya Lin and Saya Pwa—who belonged to my grandfather's world, coming to lecture every day in the purest Burmese but never noticing the existence of the modern college, its young inhabitants or other branches of learning. They were regarded with so much veneration that no student ever answered the now universally adopted English "Present" to their roll-call but replied: *"Shi ba tè, Saya:* I am here, please, Master."

At one time Saya Lin's junior Bachelor classes contained a girl student who was admired by a young man called Maung Chan Tha (which name means "Prosperity"). Maung Chan Tha had passed his junior Bachelor year and was in a senior class, but he attended the junior class daily in order to have a back view of his loved one, whom he did not dare to address. This dumb worship occasioned a daily distraction among the embarrassed girl and her companions and a lot of ribald comments from the back benches. Saya Lin continued oblivious of all this until one day the term *"paw-rana saga:* descriptive old usage," occurred in his text. "Now, shall I explain to you what *paw-rana saga* is?" said Saya Lin. "It is the other name for an object or an animal, which must describe its qualities. We have the pig, which in paw-rana may be termed *to-pwa:* prolific increase; and then we have the ox." "The ox," said the old man with a fierce denouncing arm pointed at the offending swain, "may be termed Prosperity— *Chan Tha!"* At which a hundred lusty throats yelled "Point! Point!" and the discomfited Maung Chan Tha fled, never to attend a junior class again.

When the strikers of 1936 attacked the moral influence of a young member of the staff, one of the eighteen serious charges they formally laid to his account was his habit of punning with the names of young lady students in too playful a manner. Among his students were two pretty sisters whose names, A-si and A-yi, could mean respectively, "in a row" and "smiling," a Christian girl called Margaret who was serious enough but whose name pronounced in Burmese scanned and rhymed with a word denoting excessive frivolity, and a noisy Chinese girl called Ma Ngan Chu. Said the poetic lecturer in illustrating various points:

Myet-lon galay ga ta-kyi-kyi	Little eyes, clear, beguiling,
Thwa galay ga a-si a-yi.	Little teeth, *serried, smiling.*
Kalet tet-tet	Coquette, coquette,
Mar-ga-ret.	Margaret.

Burmese proverbs

Or, in less complimentary vein:

Hsu Hsu pu pu	Boisterous shrew
Ma Ngan Chu.	Ma Ngan Chu.

But only in a novel can justice be done to the sustained humor, precision and allusiveness of colloquial speech. Proverbs may be a pointer, however, and the following, a few of the hundreds familiarly used by the normal Burman, are typical of the condensation of thought, the concrete nature of the allusions, and the witty rhyming usually present.

Kala ma-naing, *Yak-kaing mè.*	Can't get the better of the Indian, So the Arakanese is black.	Venting your wrath on a scapegoat.
Paya lè pu yin *Leiku lè tu yin.*	While worshipping at pagoda, Digging for turtle's eggs too.	Kill two birds with one stone.
Khat taing ngan-de *Pago hsa.*	O Pegu salt That flavors every ladleful.	The ubiquitous person.
Hsin pa-sat *Hnan-pet.*	Pelting the elephant's mouth With sesame seeds.	Five loaves and two fishes.
Kala taik *Kya win kaik.*	Into Indian building Tiger enters and bites.	Bedlam.
Mi-gyaung min *Yay gin pya.*	Showing the crocodile King The water tracks.	Teach Grandmother to suck eggs.

Thay yin myay gyi *Nay yin shway hti.*	Die, the earth; Stay, the gold um- brella.	Do or die. Be corpse or King.
Taung hma a-kut *Meinma hma a-wut.*	As border to basket So dress to a woman.	
Shin bayin tahka *htwet* *Pe-gyi ta-lay kyet.*	One appearance of a King, One boatload of broadbeans can be cooked.	Person who is al- ways late in ap- pearing dressed.

chapter 9

War clouds—return from England—Rangoon—shopping for clothes—bazaar girls—Chinese merchants—night bazaars—cinemas—Burmese jazz—books and newspapers—horse and boat racing—betting

After a stay of three years in England, I set out on a return journey home with a band of friends and compatriots. This was in August 1940, and the long sea voyage round the Cape gave us time for all the thoughts which filled our minds at the prospect of seeing Burma again after three and four years abroad. Besides our excitement at the approach of family reunions and the delights of once again eating Burmese food, we wondered whether the events in the outside world during the past few years, and the outbreak of the European war, had filled our people with interest, excitement or alarm for international events.

Before I left Burma I had been a student among companions who had only a passing interest in affairs outside Burma, so filled had our minds been with separation from India in 1936, the general elections for the first House of Representatives in Burma's history, the formation of the first Ministry under Dr. Ba Maw, student strikes for the amendment of the University Act, and the fervid chastising campaigns on the part of monks and fanatic students for the wearing of thick homespun by women instead of the scandalously transparent imported muslins. The older people at home also turned their eyes along the same channels. Of Hitler and Mussolini our aunts had heard, as of caricatured figures on a distant screen, and Ba Maw's admiration of Hitler's position of power was obscured by his eccentric passion for gorgeous attire, which was much more in the public eye.

The letters which I received from friends in Burma during my three years in England had also been too full of the Indian-Burman riots which raged violently in 1938, the industrial strikes in the oilfields, and the repeated school and university strikes which added to the general domestic unrest of those years, to tell me much else. But since then we had read of the opening of the Burma Road as an event of world interest; later we had read with feelings of surprise, amusement and expectancy of the face-slapping, debagging and stuffing of passports into the mouth to which the Japanese had subjected Englishmen in the ports of China, as something new and startling in our time; and later still, the closing of the Burma Road at the insistence of the Japanese Government made us suddenly connect the European politics which so excited our English friends with the events in places which surrounded Burma, though not yet with Burma itself. Brought up as a complacent child of a government officer in Burma, this was the first time that I realized how we had unconsciously thought of England, the British Empire, as a permanent world force during our lifetime—a force with which we might bargain advantageously or without success, but one that our fathers and we had taken for granted for all the time that we could remember. But now we realized it as one power—leading perhaps—among other powers in the West, and we realized also the existence of Japan

164

and remembered how the Burmans who visited it always brought back stories of the beauty, progress and good manners of the country.

We left our English friends in the first half of August 1940, as they waited, braced for an invasion, to go to what they and we considered a war-free country. I was in the Ladies Room of a big restaurant in London just before I left, when the attendant who watched me wrap my longyi asked me which country I came from. "Burma," I told her. "Burma," she repeated uncertainly. "Is there a war there, Miss?" "No," I said laughing, "but there is a Road there." Yet I was only amusing myself. As we set out home, the furthest that our thoughts of war and Burma ranged, was to wonder whether the Burma Road and the recent closing of it had made people think more about Japan and China than they had done in 1937, when the outbreak of war between the two countries had caused little excitement except that some of my friends became consistent boycotters of Japanese goods. We also wondered vaguely whether trade had been affected, and whether thought and general social conditions had been stimulated with the world-shattering event of a European war, not dreaming that this was but the splash of a pebble compared to the tempest that was to follow.

Since I had left Burma, my mother and brother and sisters had settled themselves in Rangoon and I wondered how the city would seem after the big cities of the West. Rangoon is not one of the ancient cities of Burma. Its present position in the life of the country and people is a complete turnabout from its traditional place, for in days gone by it had attracted inhabitants through spiritual rather than material renown. While Pagan, Ava, Toungoo and Mandalay rose and fell in political and commercial importance, Rangoon—Dagon as it was called—continued unchangingly a seat of pilgrimage, connected with fable and divinity, forming an actual link with another world cycle that existed in the universe before this present arrangement of Mount

Myinmo, with its surrounding heavenly, earthly, and hellish regions, was formed.

For it was on the hill called Theinguttara, which now casts its shadow on the city of Rangoon with its crown of the Shwe Dagon Pagoda, that the omens for the spiritual life of this world cycle were manifested, before the last world was dissolved in chaos. On this hill five lotus buds sprang out of the earth; they opened into blossom, and from each flew a sacred bird which bore a sacred yellow robe towards the heavens. These five robes presaged the coming of five Buddhas who would guide the future world along the noble path to Nirvana. After this sign, that former world was destroyed; the present world followed, and the Buddhas appeared as foretold: Kaukathan, Gaunagong, Kathapa and Gautama, who successively attained enlightenment in this world, and whose statues now sit, each fifty feet tall and twenty feet broad, back to back in a great quadrate at the Kyaikpun Pagoda, calm and majestic as the grass grows about them and the rain washes down on their faces, awaiting the arrival of the fifth and last Buddha, after which this world cycle will be destroyed in a universal chaos. As each Buddha saw his enlightenment in this world he left a relic at the Theinguttara Hill, which had foretold his coming and which would now mark his attainment of wisdom— Kaukathan his staff, Gaunagong his water filter, Kathapa a portion of his robe, and Gautama his eight hairs which were enshrined in the first Shwe Dagon Pagoda after many perilous journeys.

But now the importance of Rangoon banishes all that into the realm of our dreams. The beginnings of trade date from about 1760 after King Alaungpaya had won a battle here and called the place *Yangon:* end of strife; but the big foreign port sprang up suddenly after 1852 when the British gained possession of it; the ships coming into its harbor from the oceans grew larger and larger, buildings followed the expanding commerce, roads and railways were built to all parts of Burma, foreigners crowded in and stamped its character, and by 1941 Rangoon had become a cosmopolitan city of over 500,000 inhabitants, more than three times larger than the next largest city in Burma and controlling over 80 per cent of its export trade.

If the Burmese Empire of former days had been a sea-power, the development of Rangoon would not have been left to this late day, for its position makes it the obvious port for the whole country, and it had many natural beauties which would have made it a fair metropolis. Twenty-one miles up from the open sea, the Rangoon River gives a broad sweep to the left and allows a frontage of over two miles for ocean shipping to anchor. The river is a continuation of the Hlaing River flowing southwards from about fifty miles north of Rangoon and this, with the Pegu River and the Pazundaung Creek, which join its waters opposite Rangoon from the right, made inland water transport also easy. The land giving on to the Rangoon River was open and flat for the layout of a fine city, with, further in, lakes and wooded hillocks, but just north of Rangoon the range of hills known as the Pegu Yomas stretched northwards for about 300 miles, dividing the valley of the Irrawaddy from that of the Sittang, both rich alluvial valleys, so that Rangoon could stretch out its arms uninterruptedly, by road and rail and water, far up these valleys, and draw down their teak, oil and other products for export.

The actual development had taken advantage of these natural points. Along the river front were several wharves which, dredged and drained carefully, could take vessels up to 8,000 tons. Back from the Strand the city was laid out in three parallel rows, roughly two miles from east to west. Cutting down across these rows to the biggest wharf area was the broad Sule Pagoda Road with the hill of the pagoda forming the natural central circus of the city. In this area of neatly laid-out streets were the shops, offices, congested city dwellings, bazaars, narrow shut-in buildings and all the appurtenances of a city; and just where the innermost parallel ended, the railway looped through, flinging one arm up to join Prome on the central Irrawaddy, the other to

Mandalay 386 miles away, and from this arm, a line down to the Tenasserim coast. Beyond the city area the residential areas and suburbs stretched—fringing the Royal Lakes just outside with big houses of rich people; nestling among the wooded hilly Golden Valley round the slopes of the Shwe Dagon Hill, the smallness of this hilly area being drawn out with the meandering of the roads, so that the Burmese named part of it *Wingaba*, a maze, which hid cool retreats like the *Nga Dat Gyi*: Five Levels Pagoda, and a tank of sacred turtles; extending miles in a pleasant garden city of newer rich bungalows till it reached the Victoria Lakes, the University Estate and the airport beyond; taking on a village character in small wooden houses of a Burmese quarter at Kemmendine, along which the Rangoon River flowed as a country river; and straggling out in less pleasant poor suburbs to the east along the Pazundaung Creek.

Over all this area, the Shwe Dagon Pagoda shone like a golden light. Theinguttara Hill, besides being an echo of the last world, is also the last spur of the Pegu Yomas chain, which gradually peters out north of Rangoon. It has been built up to about 150 feet above the surrounding area, and from this platform the Shwe Dagon Pagoda rises, from an octagonal plinth moulded into a lotus bloom turned downwards, tapering into soft encircling rings from which is moulded again a gently swelling plantain bud, the clay merging into more soft undulations which rise to the very summit in the tightest bud of all—the *seinbu*, diamond bud —forming, by a re-echoing of the lotus buds which once sprang up here, a shapely slender spire, tapering to the point of a bud and yet composed of curves and gentle fullness. The whole pagoda was covered with pure gold leaf and its summit was crowned with a delicate *hti*, an umbrella of gold on whose rings were hung gold and silver jewelled bells which tinkled with every passing breeze. The Shwe Dagon Pagoda was a beautiful and sacred thing. In the early mornings it gave a radiance to the clear air and the blue sky; in the daylight it shone forth like a blaze of gold, burning and pure; in the evenings it glowed softly as the breeze tinkled its bells, and filled the heart with a gentle sadness which is not grief but a sweet perception of unearthly things; and at night the lights flooded it to stand high and illumined above the dark wooded slopes of the hill. At all times and from all parts of Rangoon it could be seen, calm and sublime, with the same smiling look as is seen on the face of the Buddha, not smiling in the eyes or mouth but in the serene expression of inward calm.

As we landed in Rangoon we saw a great gathering of people waiting to meet us. Going abroad for years of study is still a rare enough event to be of interest to all relatives and neighbors, so that the people were assembled not only for an affectionate reunion, but also to observe in what way the stay in England might have corrupted Burmese habits. In the case of a man it is always feared that he may bring back an English wife, and it sometimes happens that a loved child who has been away for five and six years may be greeted with tears and mourning rather than expressions of joy, if he has married an English girl. The tears of mother and sisters are very heartfelt; they express shame at what the neighbors will think, sorrow at the alienation of the man and his children which must inevitably occur, and chagrin at the loss of the rich dowry which might have been procured in the marriage market.

Even when a man does not marry in England, he is strongly scrutinized for undesirable preferences in the matter of marriage arrangements. I remember the night my brother came home. It was his first evening in Burma after nine years of English schooling and University, and it was clear enough that he was neither married nor secretly engaged to an English girl. But my Ma Ma Gyi, my eldest woman cousin, who had children as old as we were, subjected him to a searching inquiry. "Set-Set," she said, calling him by his childhood name, "do you think English girls are more attractive than Burmese girls?" My brother, who had many English friends but had not noticed any Burmese girls during his few hours in Burma, tried not to answer this question. On being held to it, he said they were different from each other and could not be compared. My cousin said, "But which do *you* like better?" She was getting quite stern by this time, and my mother and we, who felt very sorry for my brother, were all praying that he would tell a lie, as we held our breath. My brother repeated with much awkwardness that the two were different; so now my cousin took his opinion for granted, and lectured him on the desirability of marrying in an orthodox Burmese manner so that he would prove himself a good son to his mother, a good brother to his young sisters, and thus give joy to the whole family. "For," said she, "our family has always commanded respect. Grandfather was a great man, and you are the only son of the youngest family of his grandchildren, and it should not be said that with us the end tapers to a point;" which is the expression for a stock which degenerates with successive generations.

In the case of a girl there was not, of course, the fear that she would bring back an English husband, but the concern that Burmese standards of morality and dignity would be affected by an unchaperoned stay in a foreign country was very great. As we landed, I remembered enough of my childhood environment to feel the eyes of elder relatives and friends on me while I tried to restrain the wild excitement and love I felt at seeing again my mother and my young sisters now grown so sweet and shy, and I noticed also that my brother had been home long enough not to kiss me in front of my aunts as he had done when he himself had first returned from England. I felt this scrutiny also when my mother took me on the round of obeisance visits during my first days at home, and it formed a complement to the visit which I had paid to each of these elder relatives and friends before I left for England three years before. Then, each had given me a lecture which contained strong injunctions to keep to the path of virtue, modesty and dignity. But these were just *son-ma saga,* admonitory words, to be received with meekness, and not a slight on the strength of my character, just as now, when, satisfied with their scrutiny, they told my mother that her womb should be layered with gold leaf (sacrilegiously using the term for the gilding of sacred objects) for having brought forth such daughters, I was not expected to take conceit.

In all the houses of friends in Rangoon, in Thaton and Ye, I went through the same ritual, but the words of the hpongyi at Thaton moved me more than any other. "Now I will tell three stories about Mi Mi Khaing," he said, and proceeded in beautiful words and a chanting flow: "You are like a young tree planted of good seed in the fertile earth. Now the tree is heavy with ripe fruit, but the boughs are tender and bend under the weight. The tree must grow carefully and steadily, so that the full fruit do not break the young bough. . . . Let your stature be measured by your shadow that is cast after the noonday sun, for your knowledge and learning are now at noonday height. So your shadow will grow longer and longer towards the setting of the day. . . . Let your merit be like a river that gathers more strength from the rain that falls about it, and grows from a stream into a great river before it joins the mighty Thammodhaya." Then he took the monk's expression off his face, and turned to me with a smile and asked in a normal speaking voice, "Do you understand the hpongyi's language after being so long as it were one human amongst a thousand monkeys?"

Chastened and fortified by such injunctions, I was ready to plunge into six months of social life before starting on the serious business of earning a living. Rangoon should have offered plenty of scope for that, according to the rhyme about the first three cities of Burma: *"Moul-a-myaing a-sa, Mandalay sa-ga, Yangon a-kywa:* Moulmein for rich eating, Mandalay for fine speaking, Rangoon for showy vanity."

The Yangon-thu were grouped in urban or verdant clusters about the city of foreigners. There were two packed streets of the more prosperous trading classes in a western quarter of Rangoon, which the municipal authorities called Edward Street and Oliphant Street, but which to every Burman had always been known as *Kon-zay Dan:* Goods Bazaar Row, and *Shwedaung*

Dan: Gold Mountain Row. Here the families lived in tightly packed unpretentious houses and did not possess Western style furniture or cars; they went to the cinema in rickshaws, but the women were loaded with valuable diamond jewelry which put many a minkadaw to shame. In the dusk of the evenings, they sat on wooden platform couches on the pavement outside each house, puffing at cheroots, calling out to neighbors and eating a variety of choice foods from the Burmese, Chinese and Indian restaurant quarter which surrounded them.

In the east of the town, separated from this area by rows of Indian and mixed streets, retired Government officers were concentrated in a block. Here the houses were substantial, the sons and daughters attended school and University in cars, and the most eligible civil servants could be obtained in marriage for daughters, but the pensioners were the type who lived in a congested neighborhood for fear of dacoits in a more open area, and whose womenfolk considered lawns and the drawing-rooms of modern bungalows a poor substitute for the access to cinema, eating houses and bazaars that a crowded part of Rangoon afforded them.

Round about the Kokine Lakes and along the main highway to Prome, however, more newly retired Burmans who entertained on chairs, laid rugs on floors and hung pictures on walls in the Western fashion, had built pleasant modern bungalows. To the west of this area, just a stone's throw from the main Prome Road, began the village of Kemmendine with its rows of small wooden houses, each with its front enclosure full of green foliage, an altar-stand jutting out on the east wall, three steps raising the first and only story a few feet off the ground, and wooden floors with one plank loose in them to allow the dust to be swept below. Kemmendine had its own bazaar, country boats on the river, and children and dogs playing on the street, just like any district towns. My *Ko Gyi,* eldest male first cousin, lived there among small traders, clerks and school teachers. There were similar colonies of Burmese in the eastern parts of Rangoon—Yegyaw,

Bahan, Tamwe and Pazundaung—but none so pleasant as Kemmendine.

When we were young, my mother's stock of household goods
bought from their places of manufacture had shown us all the
small industries of Burma. Now my sisters appeared to be as
determined to do my Rangoon shopping from the most orthodox
sources, and I learned that to fit me out with a new set of Burmese clothes required the services and the varied talents of all
communities of the cosmopolitan city. Imported silks, which were
bought for longyis in addition to native silks, were the monopoly
of merchants from Sind and Bikaner—the houses of Ramchandra,
Tejumal, Lekraj and others—who had set up windows in the
modern Scott Market of Rangoon, and whose salesmanship had
flowered in Burma into something vastly different from the non-
chalance which they display in their native land. They offered
cigarettes to casual buyers who fingered the usual run of silks,
supplemented them with sweet colored drinks from the sherbet
stall behind the shops when they went on to more expensive
satins, and if they ventured further into fine brocades and laces,
dishes of ice-cream appeared as they waited for the material to
be cut and measured.

Cotton longyis for day and night wear in the house took us to
the western Burmese quarter of Rangoon. Here, in Goods Bazaar Row, the family firm of *U Hsin-Daw Htay:* husband and
wife married in business, lived in the upper floor of their house
and stacked the lower floor with hundreds of cotton prints, made
in Japan but manufactured with such an eye to Burmese require-
ments as regards texture, colors, design and width, that these
tha-yet-htè longyis, as they were called, seemed to most people
as Burmese as Bassein umbrellas or Mandalay slippers. All over
Burma the women wore these longyis. The transplanters of the
paddy, the young servant maids in a-so-ya mins' houses, the girls
in Ye and a thousand other villages, women in bazaars and minkadaws themselves, all wore various qualities of bright tha-yet-
htè prints bought for 10 annas to Re. 1/4 a longyi length of 1¾

yards. U Hsin and Daw Htay were prosperous; we bought our longyis from them through snobbery, in lots of ten, sitting barefooted on their mat-covered floor, with betel box in front of us, but it was possible to buy tha-yet-htè from the stalls of young Burmese women all along the big Soortee Bazaar and the Scott Market of the Town. These young women form one of Burma's fairest sights.

In the days of my schooling, when each new term plunged me into the foreign world behind convent walls, as my mother completed the shopping for it on the last day of each vacation, I gazed back with longing and envy at these fair creatures who continued work and home in one long pleasant Burmese continuity. They are girls from the ages of sixteen upward. Probably their parents set them up in these stalls, each separated from its neighbor by a stack of cotton bales, six or seven stalls on a long platform. They come there in the mornings, dressed in crisp muslin jackets and bright longyis, their faces powdered with thanakha and the Five B's, flowers in their hair, and fragrant ground bark on their hands and feet. They open up shop and dust with feather brooms while they shout across to each other the news of the previous evening. Then the whole day unfolds, calling out to food sellers and treating their friends to a succession of delicacies, button-holing the young boy who hawks magazines and tuppenny novels, and reclining against a pile of the tha-yet-hte longyis to read these romances, helping each other to fold up the pieces after a troublesome customer has gone, anything but making an earnest business of their profession. They always looked so cool and pretty and indifferent beside the small Indian storekeepers who flanked their platforms and solicited passers-by for patronage. "Oh to be a bazaar girl!" I still thought when I was in the University; "to pass unchaperoned days, reading novels and eating sweets, to have time to be powdered and neatly dressed, and only now and then be disturbed by someone who wants to buy a longyi."

Our starched white muslin jackets are made out of fine transparent muslin manufactured in England, and sent out in bales of 11 yards with the quality stamped in Burmese characters, and on the jacket a florid illustration of the quality-name—names such as *Nat-thami, Sein ta-hsok, Shwe Pan-gaing, Mè Nyo:* Heavenly Damsel, Cluster of Diamonds, Golden Spray of Flowers, Dusky Maiden—and imported by both Indian and Burmese traders.

The making up of the jackets was the monopoly of Chinese tailors; our *tayok-kalay,* little Chinese, lived in the crowded quarter of Yegyaw in a barnlike room which was carpenter's shop at one end and tailor's at the other. The tailor's end had a row of shelves along the wall into which the finished garments and uncut material were shoved, higgledy-piggledy in paper bags on which the merest scribble denoted owner and date of order. In front of this was the counter on which the cutter was at work, and separating it from the carpentry end was a table at which one or two half-clad men always seemed to be eating noodles or reading a Chinese newspaper, of which there were three in Rangoon. In spite of this, the tayok-kalay never confused an order for garments which had to fit so meticulously and always delivered them in a snow-white condition. He charged 9 annas for each fine handsewn garment, and for modern girls managed to cut twelve out of the eleven-yard piece. This was sweated labor indeed. Possibly he paid the cutter two pice, the seamstress three annas, the button-loop maker two annas, for each garment. We met one of the button-loop makers one evening as she brought a pile of finished garments, a Chinese girl of ten years, with eyes which looked tired from two years of exquisite hemming on the ten button loops of each Burmese jacket, nine jackets each day. When we had got our jackets the tayok-kalay added up our three bills into one on his abacus. Presently he announced a total of Rs. 15/5, a sum which my sisters had arrived at long before by mental arithmetic and had, in vain, been trying to thrust on his notice.

I needed also a superior quality comb to wind my hair around in a knot at the back of my head, having given away the old one

I had as a curiosity in England. My mother took me to the west
end of Rangoon, where the Chinese community are concentrated
in about six or seven streets, mostly narrow streets of three-
storied houses packed closely together, containing valuable ivory
and mother-of-pearl inlaid chairs within and jewellery behind safe
doors, but bordering deep and dirty drains and congestion in the
street. These were houses of rich men who got their money from
trading in indigenous products; by long years of industry building up large fortunes from the supplying of onions, coconuts,
potatoes and other dry goods to the retail shops in bazaars. In
the Strand running along the south end of these streets, and in
the broad Latter Street in the center of the quarter, were the big
emporiums of these traders.

One of my father's greatest friends, U Chein Swan, was a
Burma Chinese of this description, and we stayed for short periods in his three-storied house in 20th Street when we were
children. With great hospitality they gave our family one floor to
put up in whenever we came; they were ten times richer than
we, but I never decided whether my days there were more filled
with shrinking or with enjoyment. The trays of a myriad red and
yellow cakes which were spread before our eyes fascinated me
while I was in terror that I would slip into the muddy drain
beside which the cake-seller set his tray; the opalescent lights of
the mother-of-pearl chairs felt cool and smooth as I stroked them
until I suddenly turned and met the stare from the Confucian
gentlemen on the wall, with trailing mustaches and Chinese eyes;
and the wonder which I felt at the beauty of U Chein Swan's
fair daughters with their sparkling diamonds round neck and
wrists was tinged with horror at what my nurses made of an
orthodox Chinese marriage—the uncanny music, they said, the
heavy clothes, and the wedding meal would be followed by the
bride belonging for ever to the clan of her husband.

In search of a comb, however, we went to more humble streets
where my mother knew the Sino-Burmese comb sellers. The lady
of the house came running out of the kitchen as soon as she

heard us, set fruit and cool drinks before us and gossiped while she sent for the virgin sheets of tortoise shell. We held them to the light, and picked out the particular area which had the prettiest markings; discussed the shape and size and thickness of the comb and the best arrangement for the honey and brown markings. All this my mother wanted her to do for Rs. 5/- but the lady laughed and wheedled her for six rupees because, she said, sailors had had to go as far as Java to get some of her shells.

Although gold work is still given to Burmese goldsmiths in preference to any other, the trade in diamonds is not in Burmese hands. Rangoon dwellers went to buy their diamonds at Moghul Street, where a whole row of Hindu jewelers set up shop fronts and interiors in which high-powered electric bulbs, mirrors upon mirrors, technicolor photographs of the heads of the houses and of Hindu gods, all combined to make an unutterably gaudy display. Still, we took off our slippers on the threshold of these shops, and talked with great respect to the *Bagugyi,* who faced a us across a velvet padded counter on the floor.

Now I only needed buttons to hold the loops of my jackets together. Except for the occasions when diamond buttons or gold filigree-work buttons are worn, the ordinary Burmese woman wears colored buttons of cut glass or stone to match her longyi. For the poorest classes, glass buttons imported from Czechoslovakia could be bought at 2 or 3 annas a set of five, complete with glass rings to slip into the loops. But these were indeed glassy and did not last long. In Mandalay were the expert Burmese cutters, who for anything from six annas to Rs. 5 produced buttons of every description, plain, speckled, striped; of glass, semi-precious stones, or gold dust, all cut with many tiny facets. We once had in our house a heavy glass vase, imported by an English firm, of a dull bluish-black color. One day a wind mercifully blew the vase on to the floor, where it broke into a hundred pieces. My cousin gathered up the pieces and the next time she went to Mandalay her button cutter fashioned them into several sets of round sparkling buttons catching the light and showing now black, now grey, now blue, one set of which I wear to this day. These and the velvet slippers which are universally worn were sold in the market by young Burmese women sitting opposite the tha-yet-htè longyi sellers. The slippers also came from Mandalay, and in the days of the last Burmese king, the common people were forbidden to wear them; they were reserved for royal use alone.

At last my sisters considered that I was suitably dressed as the elder sister of such fashionable young ladies as they had now grown into, and equipped to attend any social function of the town. Although Burmese people love gathering to eat and drink, hotels and restaurants did not exist in Rangoon society. Both the Western restaurants where people danced and drank alcoholic drinks, and the leading Chinese restaurants where the dolled-up Chinese waitresses served the male customers with playful attentions, were out of bounds for Burmese women, and therefore not greatly frequented by Burmese men either, except in the case of the Chinese hotels as a carousal. Night bazaars were, however, eminently respectable, all Rangoon families being addicted to the habit of eating out as a supper after their dinner at home. They drove in cars to the pavement stalls of Chinatown, Moghul Street and Yegyaw; at Burmese stalls they got out and squatted on the benches provided, while the seller served them from the cooking pot beside her; at Indian and Chinese shops they had a plank thrust through to rest on the doors of the car, and ate sitting there. After eating rich Mohammedan food or delicious Chinese dishes, they drove a few streets further on to eat in the same fashion at an ice-cream or sherbet stall. It was a good life indeed.

We usually did this after the cinema. While we went to see American films, my mother and her friends invariably went to a Burmese film. There were four Burmese cinema halls in Rangoon, whose box offices were always besieged, but in spite of this the cinema industry in Burma was not a thriving one. Actors and actresses were poor and suffered a social stigma. About twenty-five feature films were produced in Rangoon each year, both sound and silent, by companies whose prosperity never lasted more than a few years. They could often be seen filming their outdoor scenes round the Royal Lakes, the University Estate and the fields around Mingaladon, using studios only for indoor scenes. In spite of this, the effects aimed at were ambitious, especially in the earlier days when the themes were from mythology and legend rather than modern streets, thus necessitating flights through the air, chariots in the clouds, magical transformations, magnificences of palaces and celestial gardens lighted by the moon. Now the films go in largely for themes of real life, but the actors and actresses still do not set the standard for everyday dress and behavior as they do in the West. A cinema actress, even when playing the part of a girl of most respectable parents, was rendered attractive by touches which in real life were considered by my mother to be suggestive of loose behavior—her hair was over-decked with flowers, her garments had floral designs, her forehead was bordered with a fringe, and the neck of her jacket fitted loosely. On the screen, however, my mother and aunts watched this enthralled. They liked also the way that love was shown, concentrating on sentimentality rather than sex. There was no kissing or attracting attention to the body, but oh the pining, the sighing, the stamping of feet, the coyness and the moonlight gazing of Burmese cinema heroines. No wonder that aunts, who once in a long while accompanied us to an American film, looked all around during the passionate kissing scenes, with scrutiny of our reaction to such displays of what should not be admitted to exist.

If the Burmese cinema failed to draw the crowd of young English-speaking men and women away from the Hollywood films, Burmese rendering of jazz conquered them completely and gave them no acquaintance with the originals from America and England. There was a body of modern songs in the true Burmese style which, unlike the old classical songs, could be sung with ease by the untrained voice, but despite this Burma did not

escape the craze which has grown up in all countries of the Far
East for snatching up tunes written in America and England and
putting them to words in the native tongue. Still, Burmans of
fastidious taste might object to the lack of music in the tunes,
rather than to the words of these popular songs, for the Burmese
words are never so execrable as the original English composi-
tions; often there is real wit, poetic brevity, and even philosophic
comment. The technique was to take the refrain of a Western
jazz tune as the repetitive theme, with a slight alteration in the
rhythm, and to embroider this extensively with a slapdash quality of Burmese turns of melody. The theme of the Burmese version probably bore no relation to that of the original. For example, the sickly account of a romantic meeting in the Isle of Capri
was converted into a satirical skit on the Rangoon fashion of
giving garden tea-parties in the English manner. Whereas the
Burmese custom at weddings and other celebrations in the country towns was to invite townspeople to a full meal, with the
feasting of monks and the distribution of gifts, the Yangonthu
had taken to employing the catering services of Western-style
restaurants to bring chairs, tables, food and attendants for the
sum of Re. 1/4 per head. The tune which was written to sing
sentimentally of the Isle of Capri now sang, with romping glee,
the English names of these delicacies:

> Vi-ta-mo, co-co *hnin amyo son myi*
> Ham pattie, cream roll *hnin* cold coff-ee,
> Columbia *dat pya hnin htè hso myi,*
> Plain cake *hnin* Gold Flake *le kyamma wè myi.*
> Etc.........

> Vitamo, cocoa and all kinds you'll see,
> Ham patties, cream rolls and cold coffee,
> With Columbia record playing merrily,
> Plain cake and Gold Flake will I buy for tea.

> Expensive things, expensive things of all kinds for eating,

> I'll order from a restaurant for this fashion meeting,
> Sit up round a table in gathering so hearty,
> A very respectable tea-drinking party.

> Don't eat of Burmese comestibles,
> They are so indigestible.

On the other hand the lilting tune of the Campdown Races was slowed down to sing:

> *Chit-te thu ko twap hma tha,*
> *Seik pyaw,*
> *Aye da.*

> Only when you see the loved one,
> Heart is happy,
> Mind at rest.

Compared to dwellers of country towns, Yangonthu not only went to the cinema oftener, but also read a good deal more, probably in the absence of so many happy-eating-gatherings and charity feasts. There were four daily newspapers in Burmese and a few which appeared bi- or tri-weekly. The daily paper provided a lot of reading matter for the average person; a grand-aunt of mine made it a daily institution to sit on her verandah with a bottle of lemonade and the *New Light of Burma,* whose twenty-four pages were filled with international news, home politics, articles on the economic development of the country and attacks on abuses prevalent in social life, exhortations to good behavior to the younger generation, reports of cases of a scandalous nature, just like a popular daily anywhere in the world. But in Burma there was no distinction such as exists between a paper which tries to keep a dignified face, like the London *Times,* and papers which make sensational interest their strong point. Similarly, poetry and clear prose were not the monopoly of a class of intellectuals, although certain periodicals such as the

World of Books endeavored to contain only literary excellence; wit and vivid description could be present in the tuppenny novels. These two-anna novels were largely drug-like and pornographic in nature. There was a great trade in them, about 30,000 being sold annually in Rangoon. Mobile circulating libraries functioned in the person of hawker boys who went round to houses, selling them at two annas each, returning the next week to buy the used copies back for one anna and selling a fresh lot. They also brought monthly magazines containing articles on a fairly wide variety of subjects. The following is a sample of the contents of one such popular magazine—costing 8 annas and read by all who read the tuppenny novels—*Kyi-Pwa-Yay, Progress-Prosperity,* for September 1941.

Title	Description
Don't Fear War	Wars are in the natural order of things, and we must not fear them but be ready to encounter them.
The Myook	Comic verse.
Love and Vanity	Translation of English story with a moral.
Inscriptions of Pagan Period	Descriptive account of inscriptions in Pagan.
Win on Every Throw	Short story, set in gaming houses of Chinese quarter of Rangoon.
The True Burman	Instalment of series on muscular development.
Two Blossoms	Short story of a doctor's family in country town.
Impermanence of States and Races	Warning that the Burmese race may die out with wholesale settling of foreigners.
Biggest of Their Kind	Information tid-bits.
Miss Fiery Temper	Love story of a bazaar girl.
Tour in Arakan	Factual and humorous account of visit to Arakan.

Horse-racing in Rangoon was a foreign importation, but nevertheless the stadium was always filled, not only with the fashionable section in an enclosure but also with rows of four-anna spectators who had been collected from all the streets of the town by the privately-run Burmese buses which tore along on race days, with two "spares" (spare-men in addition to the driver) hanging out from the back step and shouting to all they passed: "Race-a-ko! Race-a-ko! Race-course, race-course." But in the country the traditional boat racing was still alive. Boat races were held in every village which had a stream or river, as an annual event after the Lenten season. Long narrow canoes built in the village itself were rowed by twenty-two men and put out in rivalry between quarter and quarter, or between one village and another. At Ye the upper street and lower street put out boats bearing names of prowess or aquatic grace. The cheering and betting raged more furious and wild with the manner of the finish: the winning post was a boat in the center of the stream, equidistant from the tracks of each boat, and across this was laid a hollow cane sticking about three feet out on either side. Through the hollow was thrust the prize *pan:* flower (of victory), a stick with a flag on each end. The winning crew was to seize this flower before it could be called victorious, and thus a dead-heat often sent both crews tumbling into the water as they wrestled for the prize.

Burmans are said to have an irrepressible gambling spirit, even when no money is laid on. A stock example, quoted by foreigners, of the Burman's readiness with a dah in his hot temper gives as provocation the anger worked up between two men who sit idly

in a tea-shop, and for lack of amusement bet on the number of
flies which will settle on the sugar bowl. I prefer the story of two
street urchins who saw two monks walking before them sedately,
with downcast eyes and steady pace, as monks should walk.
"Look," says one idle urchin, "there are two hpongyis. You look
at the one on the right, I'll watch the one on the left. I bet you
my hpongyi walks faster than your hpongyi." The monks ignore
this, but soon begin to hear: "My holiness is going faster!" "No,
mine!" Unobtrusively, each hyongyi tries to walker quicker and
yet with dignity. The boys get thoroughly excited now. "*My*
holiness!" "No, *my* holiness!" Soon the astonished spectators see
two hpongyis running with unholy energy and two small boys
streaking after them shouting: "My hpongyi! Hey, my hpongyi!"

chapter 10

My brother's wedding—festivals and rites—war comes to Burma

THE showy vanity of Rangoon was seen at its greatest at wedding celebrations, where no woman of any standing came without a full load of jewellery, either owned or borrowed for the occasion. For weddings of families like ours hundreds of invitations had always to be sent out owing to the tradition of acknowledging distant relationships and connections. It would be considered rude also not to invite the friends among clerks and traders from every town in which my father had been posted during our growing-up years.

Marriage is a social contract in Burma. To be married one needs no recourse to legal or priestly officers. The *let-htat*, laying of hands one on the other, can be performed in the presence of elders, or a feast can be given to a few people to obtain recognition of the married state. This is done after elopements, for example, when the parents have become reconciled and the young couple is too shy to go through the pantomime of a marriage ceremony. For divorce, also, no legal procedure is necessary, but convention makes divorce rare. Although monogamy is almost universal in Burma, polygamy is not forbidden by the law. A "mistress" of a married man is considered a sort of wife, but the disapproval with which this is regarded is shown in the term applied to her: *ma-ya-nga,* lesser wife. But the liberty operates both ways, and in the rare cases of a woman who runs to a second husband without any agreement having been reached beforehand, she is said to have a *lin-ngè,* lesser husband. The lack of legal safeguards of a woman's position as the only wife is amply compensated for by the rulings of Burmese Buddhist law as regards her property. She retains sole ownership of whatever property she brings to the marriage, and on the dissolution of the marriage is entitled to half of all the additions of wealth since the marriage. Neither can an irate husband make a will leaving his money to other relatives and strangers. Wills are forbidden by law; children inherit equal shares of the parents' legacy, except in the cases where there are more than four children in the family. Then the eldest takes one-quarter before the rest is divided equally among the other children. On the death of one parent the surviving parent still has sole ownership of half the property. The other half is open to division among the children, but it is only a black sheep who will insist on division while one parent is still alive.

When I had been home but a month, my brother appealed to me for help in arranging the matter of his marriage. His difficulty was that he had no wish to marry the various dowried young women with whom my relatives were trying to contract him; he had chosen his own bride but at the same time the stern array of cousins, aunts and uncles in our family made it necessary to arrange things in a traditional manner. My brother had chosen his bride from a family of sisters who had been to school with us and with whom we were on the friendliest terms, so that he could have pressed his own suit if he wished, but since my sister-in-law's family also stood for tradition, we had to go through elaborate negotiations.

For a go-between we chose a lady who belonged to high circles of Rangoon society and who was known to be a great friend of the girl's family. One morning my mother and I paid her a formal call and made the proposal, my mother reciting the list of her son's qualifications, which the lady already knew quite well. She promised to approach the guardian aunt of the girl's family. Shortly after this, we called on the aunt, who demurred, not to seem eager, and said, moreover, that she could not give an answer until she had consulted an astrologer to see whether the stars of the young man and woman formed an auspicious union. We thereupon gave her the date and hour of my brother's birth. During all this time, no word had passed between my future sister-in-law and us upon the matter; we did not, in fact, visit her. In due course, the aunt gave her answer, and while my brother was out of town on a tour, a party was held at the girl's house, with the senior relatives of both sides present to formalize the engagement. No unmarried young girls should attend this, out of modesty, and although I went along as my mother's right-hand, I had to closet myself in the bedroom with the girls. It was only then, when the elders were formalizing the engagement, that my sister-in-law did not feel it forward to talk about the wedding and future happiness with much excitement. After the engagement had been announced, my brother was allowed to call every day during the three months of their engagement, but they were not allowed to be seen together in public.

Meanwhile, great preparations went on, for besides the social arrangements attendant on all weddings, the attire of the bride and bridegroom had to be matched in color, a panegyric writer had to be found to write the poem of praise, and suitable elders to perform the ceremony had to be agreed upon. The modern Burmese custom is to ask the most respected highly-placed Burmese couple among the family's friends, along with an equally respected English official to pronounce recognition in English.

This learning of English by a vast number of Burmans, and their daily activities in that language, have led to much duplication of effort in the disposal of their spirits also. When a person is buried, a notice is served on his spirit that this body is now to be vacated, and the spirit to go elsewhere for fear that the faithful spirit hovering round the grave may create a ta-say, a ghost. When a student died in term-time at the University, the rites at her funeral were completed only when a lecturer went to the head of the grave and said in English: "So-and-so, I give you notice that you are no longer in the Jr. B. A. class." When U Tin Gyi died during an official visit to England, we held his cremation at Golders Green and succeeded in getting a Singhalese hpongyi from the Buddhist Lodge in London to perform the rites. In spite of the environment of the crematorium we felt that we had achieved a dim and religious Buddhist atmosphere, such as he would have wished, by the time the hpongyi had intoned the verses, with all the gathered Burmese students repeating them phrase by phrase. But suddenly one of the English officers present got up and read in English: "U Tin Gyi, O.B.E., Registrar for Co-operative Societies in the Government of Burma, I give you leave to relinquish your post in the service of the Government. Signed—Adams." As if the persistent ghost might return to haunt in English, having been dismissed in only one of his two languages.

Mr. Bernard Swithinbank of the I.C.S. had, through long years of friendship for Burmese people, laid the hands of many young couples one upon the other in marriage, and in this case he seemed particularly fitted for the task, for twenty-five years before he had married the parents of the bride, and though he could not perform for the bridegroom's parents their marriage ceremony, which was held in Grandfather's time, it was he who gave my father leave to go to Thaton, as senior officer wishing him all prosperity in his marriage.

At last the great day arrived and all the male cousins and

uncles collected at our house to dress the bridegroom with as much fuss as attends a bride in any other country. My mother had bought three pink silk turbans varying barely perceptibly in shade, so that the young man's complexion might be matched exactly when the fateful hour approached. My two young sisters and I took one each and sewed the finest possible seams, but submitting every inch as we went along to the scrutiny of my senior uncle, Kyaw Din, who said that a man's turban needed finer sewing than any woman's garment. My *Ko Lay*, most debonair of the cousins, tied the turban on my brother's head, while the band of elder brothers-once-removed stood around and complained that he did not make the floating end dance and toss with sufficient sprightliness. Two uncles and two cousins combined to tie his *pasoe*, the magnificent skirt which had been brought down from Mandalay and matched in the weaving with the bride's own skirt. My brother submitted to all of this with a meekness born of never having worn full Burmese dress before. All the while my three sisters danced around to look at him from every angle, exclaiming with sauciness and delight how beautiful and pink he looked, for my brother was really a robust and dark-skinned type of man who liked to wear sober English clothes.

When we arrived in procession at the bride's house, we found all her relatives gathered in the drawing-room, men down one side and women down the other; at the head a couch for the presiding elders, U Maung Maung and Mr. Swithinbank, before it a pair of rich cushions for the bridal pair to sit upon, and before it again a giant bowl of carved silver, filled with flowers and offerings. Everything in here was silent, restrained and correct. None but relatives were present, not divorcees, nor those whose married lives had been scandalous, lest they spoil the auspicious nature of the day.

I slipped into the bedroom to see the bride and, pausing, caught my breath to see how lovely she looked at that moment. On her wedding-day a Burmese woman wears the full court-dress of the bygone days of the Burmese kings; the dress was worn by the queens and princesses of our songs and history, as they bowed before the magnificence of the king on his throne, as they stood by casements in the moonlight, as they sang songs of melancholy when evil days were upon them and their enemies had prevailed over them. The long side tress, the trailing open skirt, the tight jacket which left the bosom bare for necklaces of diamonds, were created to show the perfections of a beautiful woman. Neither tall nor short should she be, her waist small and her breast carried high, her skin smooth and yellow like the thanakha finely ground, rich and creamy, her eyes like those of a golden doe, beneath eyebrows arched no heavier than a three days' moon, her lips two ruby gems, and her hair as black as a beetle's wings. Such was Ommadhanti, such Pabhawadi, the beautiful one. Such was my sister-in-law on that day as she came out, betraying no emotion and recognizing no one as she walked up the room in silence and sank down on the cushion beside the bridegroom.

Now the writer of the panegyric rose and chanted the paean of praise. The young *tha-do-tha*, Maung Sett Khaing, so blessed with virtues, complete with every manly quality; the young *tha-do-thami*, Khin Khin Su, so beautiful and full of womanly dignity; both of good race, good stock, to be married thus auspiciously, to have a good long life together, so great is their merit. Then the elder presiding lady put the offerings from the silver bowl, one after another, into the hands of the bride, and she made obeisance with each one. Now was every evil banished and every good present, for the performance of the *mingala,* the auspicious thing. The bridal pair rose from the cushions and took their places on the couch; U Maung Maung took the hands of bride and groom, laid them one upon the other, and dipped them into a golden bowl of water as the reader of the panegyric now called witness to the marriage. Then Mr. Swithinbank held their hands together and said in English: "Maung Sett Khaing and Khin Khin Su, I pronounce you man and wife."

All this was a solemn affair; there were no music, no speeches,

no outsiders, and no photographs; but by the end of the ceremony murmurs of the activity in the garden floated in. There, a
tea-party such as the song recounts was being arranged, with an
orchestra, Indian waiters, photographers and young men in bright
longyis to usher the guests around. After the tea, the wedding
guests went to see not so much the presents which were laid out
on tables, but the bridal chamber, fitted with richest trappings,
and guarded against male intrusion by a gold thread across the
door, to break across which the men must pay in gold. All the
guests now streamed into this chamber, the women peering here
and there, lifting the coverlet of the bed to see if the traditional
blankets of velvet were present, prodding the softness of the
mattress, estimating the taste of the bride in the choice of fine
linen and lace hangings. The custom is for the pair to spend their
first days in this chamber in the house of the bride's family, before they go to live in their own house.

Different though the life in Rangoon was from the days in the
districts, our Buddhist festivals still came round for social gathering and celebration. In a big town, however, with electricity,
crowded streets and cars, the celebrations tended to stand out
more as night celebrations. Pagoda festivals at any of the pagodas
in the suburbs drew a procession of cars and buses to the right
bazaars, anyeins, and the light points twinkling out of the surrounding blackness. But these twinkling lights were mutiplied a
thousandfold at the lighting-up festivals, of which we had two.
Thadingyut, or the release from Lenten sobriety, ushers in the
springtime of the year: now may all weddings, shinbyus and
ear-borings take place, now may fasting days decrease and the
full moons of lighting and harvesting and the new year water-
play follow before another Lent; the deluge of the rains has
ceased at last, the sky has been washed blue and the air blows
cool and gentle. At Thadingyut, all houses light up their verandahs and gardens; streets of houses put up pavilions and offer
food and stage shows to all the townspeople who ride along in

cars, trams and rickshaws to look at the lights from end to end of the town.

During my last Thadingyut in Burma we had a happier idea. Leaving our house with a nominal number of oil-flame dishes burning, we went in a party of twelve to the hill of the Shwe Dagon, to light there one thousand candles as our magnificent deed of merit. We walked up the western approach, a covered way of pillars and stalls selling fragrant flowers, incense sticks and candles for offering; barefooted up steps which we came to sweep at other times in the belief that this good deed brings the doer the beauty of long and black hair in the next existence. From a number of stalls we bought our thousand candles—thin white candles made for us and for export, in the Syriam refinery across the river, from the petroleum of Burma's oilfields. Our arms laden with these packets, we emerged on to the open, marble-paved platform from which the Shwe Dagon rose, surrounded by images, miniature pagodas and shrines in an encircling row. Along the circumference of the paved platform were big trees and rest houses where people kept sabbath, or reclined during a quiet day of eating and meditation.

We chose a spot free from other worshippers and said our prayers. Then we began the lighting; each of us on a space two feet long, taking fire from the neighboring lights of other offerings for the first candles, setting them down on the stone ledge encircling the shrines, and fixing the bases of row upon row from the fire of the beacon candle, until they overflowed onto the marble floor. How pretty they looked, those straight white unlit sticks, so regular in the dim light. Then we took a torch candle and used it as a taper, touching each stick into life; but the struggle of it, with the wind blowing so high on the hill, and a strong gust knocking down the infirm ones, and other candles lighting quicker than one's own, and the young children poaching on each other's rows and stealing fire, exciting us all as one after another each act of merit twinkled into light, until the last rows were done in time to have all thousand candles burning together in a beautiful bright offering.

The Thadingyut moon, on waning, was followed by the Tasaungmon, and when that moon grew full, the town was lighted up again. This time it was to commemorate the return of Gautama from his visit to Tawadeintha, the region of heavenly spirits into which his mother Maia had been reincarnated after her death on this earth. When I was very young we had a lesson about how, after attaining enlightenment, the Blessed One wished that his mother could hear the wisdom which he now possessed, how he journeyed up the Tawadeintha Mount to preach to her, and how, on his return, the monks and holy men of that region lighted his descent back to earth, holding tapers out of the gloom in two rows, on either side of him. As a child I dreamed of this as a wondrous vision; I pictured the space between the two worlds as black as only a void can be, not to be crossed by any means except the divine or the celestial, and I pictured the glowing tapers making a continuous ray of gold across this deep blackness, lighting up the yellow robes of the Holy Order and the face of the Buddha in its beatitude.

But the lighting up at Tasaungdaing is all tinsel and glitter; in Rangoon it was done with much more festivity than at Thadingyut. In the University every Buddhist student subscribed towards lighting up in rivalry between halls—lanterns and oil-flame dishes were arrayed along all verandahs, trees, window-sills and gateways, the façade of the hall bearing a giant lantern in the shape of the Buddha. In the town the gayest display was put on by the trader residents of Gold Mountain and Goods Bazaar Rows. These people, who cared not for races, garden tea-parties nor fashionable weddings, put all their zest into the Tasaungdaing celebration. Each entrance to the streets was spanned with arch and pavilion, and between the two ends were contained lights, feeding at each house, a stage show, arrays of presents which were being offered to monasteries, and a jostling mass of people from all parts of the town. Among all the glitter moved

the daughters of the houses, also on display; their breasts sparkling with the full stock of jewellery, the diamond spangles in
their hair trembling in scintillation like the quivering balls of
silver and tinsel on the decorations around them.

All this tinsel and glitter, sparkle and glistening tintillation
reached its crowning point, only to be shown as vanity, fantasy,
in the spectacle put forth at the cremation of a revered hpongyi—
one whose life on the earth was all austerity and solidity of the
worth of gold. A monk dies and is embalmed in honey and put
to lie in state for perhaps a year, while the *lu*, ordinary humans,
prepare for the cremation that is to send him off on his return
flight to higher states of existence. He whose life has been lived
in accordance with the belief that all earthly things, all ornament
and pleasures of the earth, are illusion, impermanence and struggle, now has his exit prepared for by weaker mortals who build
and decorate a seven-tiered pavilion for his pyre; and fantastic
mammoth creatures to flank it high in the sky—giant birds, tigers
and elephants, high on the slopes of Shwe Dagon Hill, tall and
gigantic, but empty within, of inflammable bamboo and paper,
caparisoned with gaudy, floating trimmings. Under the vast
shadows of these empty creatures gay pavilions for feeding and
the sale of bright ware are put up, lights are festooned for a night
bazaar. When the day dawns for the burning, crowds throng to
the fair, in merriment because the monk who so long ago re-
nounced his attachment to human affections leaves no grieving
widow and children; the coffin is lifted into its tiered catafalque
and laid on a bed of inflammable tinder; it is drawn to the center
of the giant animals. When the feasting, buying and jostling have
had their run, word passes round that the final moment is about
to take place; people are drawn towards the canopy; the masters
of ceremony throw rockets and torches into the decked bier;
four, five and suddenly a hundred tongues of fire lick the bamboo, paper and the bed of tinder, and a magnificent blaze rises
into the sky. Soon other torches set aflame the row of animals,
and elephants, tigers, boats and birds go up in smoke, together

with canopy, bier and coffin, leaving no traces of the saintly body. Excitement abates, the crowds leave the fair, the sellers their stalls, and of the caparisoned field only a charred blackness remains.

So soon the fires of war were to burn up not only the show and tinsel of Burma, but things more solid and golden than the life of a monk—rice fields and food of all kinds, *ain-daung-pyit-si,* the setting-up-house-goods of a million husbanding families, the houses, villages and towns whose peace allowed men and women to weave, cure fish, make boats, carve silver and wood and ivory, and indulge, their laughing children. December 8th fell soon after the full moon of Tasaungmon, when the Lent-free season was but short-lived, and laid a blight upon the whole country. Destruction was so swift, so sudden.

For nations which declare war or have war declared on them, the day of outbreak ushers in a grim period, but it is clear in the minds of the people that this is a call to effort and sacrifice, for the idea of nation, sovereignty, liberty, whatever they have learned to hold dear for long generations, or else have just newly won to cherish as something precious. They know, when war is declared, that they must defend their country, have ready for sacrifice their young men, and work with grim industry in a geared-up machine. But how could this apply in the case of Burma, a country which had lost proud sovereignty fifty-five years before, which had not yet gained a modern replacement for it, and which felt itself to be only incidentally in the path of the war monster's appetite. Even those of the people who had been expecting war with the rumors that flew around Rangoon for the six months previous to this, either from people who had cause to know or from a clear judgment, did not know quite how to feel when it came upon them. In our family councils as to which place would offer the best sanctuary from bombs, gunfire and the recklessness of fighting soldiery, a young cousin opposed the idea of our ancestral Thaton as being directly in the path of the invader. "Well, what if it is," said her mother; "do we go to the middle of the roadway, and stand, looking up with mouth open to receive the cannon balls? We are human beings, eating rice. We can reason like human beings and move aside, avoid a little, and the menace will go straight down the road, and after a time leave us safe behind."

This might be regarded as typical enough of the attitude of the majority of people—to move aside from big places and the scenes of war, to leave posts when to hold on to them would be snapping with jaws agape at the gunfire of a fast-winning invader. But the results of this policy was enough to fill us with wretchedness. People ran here and there, from one set of relatives to another, not always welcoming; setting out with foolish encumbrances of goods and chattels and gradually being forced to shed them piece by piece, with the bitter realization that they could not be saved. But war raged like a forest fire which creeps to the farthest corner; like a deluge which rises to the highest hill, for people went northwards and northwards, and still found no sanctuary.

Another thing that filled us with wretchedness was the feeling that all the activity of a normal life would cease. The people who thought reasonably in the face of the quick Japanese onrush, that the British would probably have to get out but would prepare, perhaps in India, and be able to return one day, expected to spend the next few years in quiet and hiding from danger. The average person just felt vaguely stunned, that now there would be a negation of all social and economic endeavor; he could not visualize any quick restoration of even a shell of the machinery of normal life which was so alarmingly disappearing before his eyes. Symbolic of this was the emptying of schools and colleges in Rangoon within the day on which the news of Pearl Harbor came through. I shall never forget the effect on my young sisters and their friends. They cried with grief as their parents came to take them home, parting them from friends, sweethearts, all companions of youth, books and the outside world, at best to go into

my evacuation from Burma

the jungle and live as though they had never known a world looking toward Europe.

I was twenty-five when war broke out, and caught me up, in late February 1942, in a compulsory sea evacuation carried out by the military authorities. I felt as though my heart would break against this awful machine which had suddenly made us so unimportant, and which did not care that I was a Burman amidst the crowd of foreign women it was evacuating, taking me from mother and sisters, to whom I could not get news or explanation of my desertion.

As we left Inya Hall with lights ablaze, fans full on, storerooms thrown wide open and waiting for the invader, a vast and inexpressible sadness settled upon me. Dawn had not yet broken, and only the glare from Kemmendine fires still lighted the sky. How sad, how black and empty each familiar house-face looked, with shut eyes and shuttered doors. It was goodbye indeed, for though the flames are dying now, we shrink from contemplating the charred desolation that we must see on our return.

But it would have been goodbye in any case for another, happier reason; for I had just met my husband, who would have carried me off to a different world in the farthermost corner of Burma, the Kengtung State of Shans, in a land of mountains, narrow valleys and pine trees, where simple people with rosy cheeks cultivate the hillsides and address the ruling family as "Heavenly," where women are not heard, but seen in meekness to obey and fear their husbands. That is another story.

glossary

a-hlus, mass cooking for free feasting, 129

a-hmway, tree whose bark is ground into a cosmetic, 49

ain-daung-pyit-si, household goods, 194

a-kyo nay, "preparing-to-greet day," New Year's Eve, 98

anyein-pwè, variety show, 152

Apana, Grandfather's Indian servant, 35

arahat, man ready to attain Nirvana, 97

a-say-hkan, servants, 44

a-sein-bok, rotten vegetation, 129

a-si-hkan, solid stub for rolling into end of cheroot, 125

a-so-ya min, Government official from Burma Civil Service Class II, 43

aung-thwe, go-between, 119

ausa, authority, 117

badamya, jewel, possession of highest worth, 83

balachaung, toast spread with *seinsa ngapi*, a dish for Europeans, 132

baw, fine silver, 51

bedin-saya, fortune teller, astrologer, 63

bein-mon, wheat cake, 136

belu, ogre, 61

bi-mon, comb cake, 136

bi-yaung-tan, combseller (a game), 59

boha-dauk, a Westerner's hair-cut, 30

bok-ta-lon tauktè, a tucktoo with a buff, i.e., blind man's buff, 61

chaung bya, stream's source, 23

cheik, elaborately patterned silk, 128

chep-paung, a kind of vegetable, 132

chet, cooked, 132

chimbaung, roselle leaves, 48

chinlon, a ball game, 32

chit, love, 118

dacoit, armed robber, 35; *dacoity*, robbery

daga, giver, 26

dah, blade, 50

dahma, heavy chopper for wood, meat, etc., 50

dalwè, knife for splitting bamboos, etc., 50

damauk, light paring knife, 51

damyaung, dagger carried by Shans, 51

dandalun, edible fruit, 39

dani, nipah tree, 88

da-nyin, a tree like a laburnum, 110

dasu-may, lit. forgotten trees, a particularly good variety of mango, 33

dat-le-ba-say, lit. "physic of the four elements," 63

daung, pounded, 132

daung-kwa-mon, peacock's hoof cake, 136

eggaya-hto, alchemy, 117

galon, an animal, 98

gangaw, flowering tree, 25

Gaung-se kyun, island in Moulmein river, 99

ga-zun-ywet, water greens, 138

gon, prestige, 117

go-nyin, seeds in children's games, 58

gwe, tree with sweet fruit, 39

gyo, cake of rice, 131

hin, curry, 130

hingyo, soup, 130

hkut-tè, ladling out, 131

hmway-dè, fragrant, 90

hna-yet, second day, 78

hnè, clarionet, 153

hpa, cane box used when travelling, 56

hpet-hpu, leaf-bud, 129

hpon, glory, holiness, 71

hpongyi-bo-sha-na, pill for coughs and sore throats, 62

hpon-nein, to lower a man's *hpon*, making him subservient to his wife, 71

glossary

hpya, reed mat, 47

hsa-nwin mak-kin, cake not free from turmeric, 136

hsay, mixture, 125

hsi-byan, oil-returns-curry, 133

hsi-mi-khwet, earthen oil-flame dishes for festival lights, 48

Hsin-byu Shin, Lord of the white elephant, 96

hsu-taung, that part of prayers in which blessings are asked for, 115

htamanè, special rice dish for festivals, 79

hti, umbrella of gold at summit of pagoda, 167

hto, making, 79

htok-si-tan, a team game, 59

kalamè, tree whose bark is ground into a cosmetic, 49

kalapè so, cake-wee-gram-balls, 136

kan, fate, luck, 64

kanazo, a sweet-sour fruit, 94

kattu, small sailing ship, 31

kaukhnyin, glutinous rice, 79

khamè, charm, 64

kha-yay, a tree from whose flowers garlands are woven, 58

kho, dove, 129

khway-yu, mad dog, the one left out in a game, 61

kinmun, a kind of tree, 131

Ko-Gyi, eldest male first cousin, 167

Ko Ko, elder brother, 118

kyauk-chaw, cake smooth as marble, 136

kyauk-ka, lacquer, 52

kyaukpyin, stone for grinding *thanakha*, 48

kyauksein, lit. "green rock," jade, 83

kyaung, monastery and school, 25

kyaungtha, scholar, 25

kyaw-gyet, fry-cook, 133

kyet-thway, cock's blood, 129

kyi-waing, instrument made with series of gongs, 55

la-hpet, pickled tea-leaf, 64

la-hsan, new moon, 78

la-hsot, waning moon, 79

la-myo shit-sè, lit. "80 kinds of wind," a digestive powder, 62

la-pyit nay, full moon day, 78

laung, dug-out boat, 53

lawba, greed for riches, 116

lay-hto-tè, wind-to-pierce, 138

lay-naing-tè, wind conquering, 138

lè, fields, 111

lè-gat, narrow gold collar, 83

lethok, lit. "hand-wiping or mixing," a kind of vegetable dish, 132

let-htat, laying of hands one on another in marriage ceremony, 184

lè-ton, necklace, 83

let-wut let-sa, lit. "wear for the arms and such," jewellery, 82

Lin-ngè, lesser husband, 185

longyi, skirt worn by both sexes, 26

lu, ordinary human beings (as opposed to a monk), 193

ma, female; odd (as opposed to even; see *son*), 59

mahanahpu, noble forehead, 126

Ma-Ma Gyi, elder sister, 91

Maung, younger brother; used as form of address by wife to husband, 118

Ma-ya-nga, lesser wife, 185

may-yan, marian seed, 129

mezali, tree with bitter leaves, 131

mi-go, smoke, 129

mingala, part of marriage ceremony, 189

minkadaw, wife of Government official, 43

minthami, dancing girl, 154

mon-baing-daung, cake in stick pieces, 136

mon-hsan, cake sprinkled, 136

mon-hsi-kyaw, cake fried in oil, 136

mon-ka-lame, black Indian cake, 136

mon-kywè-thè, buffalo's liver cake, 136

mon-le-bway, whirlwind cake, 136

mon-leit-pya, butterfly cake, 136

mon-let-kauk, bangle cake, 136

mon-lok-saung, cake made by covering, 136

mon-longyi, big-cake-ball, 136

mon-lon-yay-paw, cake-balls floating, 136

mon-pein-nè-si, jackseed cake, 136

mon-pyissa-lè, worthless cake, 136

myet-hna-gyi, "big face," someone
of importance, 117

myookship, junior Government post,
41

nadwin, ear-boring ceremony, 70

naga, dragon, 98

nat, spirit, 52

Neibban Zay, Nirvana Bazaar, 137

nethani, nethapyu, trees whose bark
is ground into a cosmetic, 49

*nga-bat, nga-gyi, nga-gyin, nga-hpa-
ma, nga-khu, nga-myin, nga-pè,*
kinds of fish, 134

ngan-say, black powder, taken to re-
duce a temperature, 62

ngapi, paste made from prawns, 90

nga-ponna, kind of fish, 134

nga-tha-lauk, kind of fish, 28

nga-the-lè-do, nga-yan, kinds of fish,
134

nyaung-bin, sacred banyan, 25

nyi-ma-lay, little sister; used as form
of address by husbands to wives,
119

ohn-nè, coconut flower, 125

ok, book, 129

ok-ta-sauk, spirit of the next world,
61

ok-tè, covering with the vegetable,
133

padauk, a flower, 101

palin, jewelled reclining chair, 73

pan, flowers, 58; flower (of victory),
182

pan-nu, tender flowers, 129

pasun-hsi, prawn oil, 129

pa-thein halawa, Bassein cake, 136

Paw-Pwa, Grandmother, 24

paya, a term of great respect, 64

payin, amber, 129

peik-ta, spirit of the next world, 61

pein, arum, 34

pè-myit, bean, 136

pinlè wa, ocean's opening, 24

pin-sin tha-ma, the word "pensioner" incorporated in Burmese,
108

po-sa, mulberry tree, 128

pulway, flute, 153

pyaw-pwè-sa, "happy-eating-gather-
ing," picnic, 67

sado, pin for the hair, 82

sadone, style of hairdressing, 126

saing-waing, musical gathering, 153

salaungbon, cover for earthen pot,
48

sameik, false tress added in hairdressing for coquetry, 127

sameik-kwin, more restrained form
of above, 127

sa-sa-ya, food eaten at a regular
meal, 135 (see *tha-yay-sa*)

saungs, stout woven cotton pieces
used as blankets, 47

saya-daw, senior monk, 25

seinbu, diamond bud at summit of
pagoda, 167

sein-pan gaing, diamond and gold
pins for the hair, 82

seinsa, diamond, 90

sètauk-tè, seed-flicking game, 59

shikko, make obeisance to or worship, 66

shinbyu, initiation ceremony for
boys, 30

shinlaung, boy attendant on monk,
73

shwe-dinga, gold sovereign; used as
a qualification of durians, 93

si, seeds, 59

son, a pair; even, 59

son-ma, witches, 61

son-ma saga, admonitory words, 169

Tabodwè, full moon festival (January-February), 79

taik-pan, Honolulu creeper flowers,
52

ta-nga-thès, fishermen; regarded as
outcasts, 90

tanya, servants' quarters, 44

glossary

ta-say, ghost, 61
ta-yet, first day, 78
ta-yok chi-thay-ma, tiny-footed Chinese women, 122
tayok-kalay, little Chinese, 146
Tegatho, University, 146
thabaw, reed, 48
Thadingyut, celebration at the end of Lent (in October), 79
tha-do-tha, bridegroom, 189
tha-do-thami, bride, 189
tha-gyan daw gyi, ceremonial washing of the King's hair at New Year, 99
tha-gyan hta-min, special cooking of rice at New Year, 102
tha-gyan mo, rain showers at New Year, 101
tha-gyan-sa, beginning of New Year, 98
thakin, master, 45
thakinma, mistress, 45
tha-na, compassion, 118
thanakha, tree whose bark is ground into a cosmetic; the paste made from this, 49
thanat, tree whose leaves are used for wrapping cheroots, 125; type of vegetable dish, 132
Thaton, town 100 miles north of Moulmein, 33
tha-yaw, fiddle tree, 99
tha-yay-sa, food eaten between meals, 135 (see *sa-sa-ya*)
tha-yet, mango, 64
tha-yet-htè, a style of *longyi,* 172
the-byay, plum, 99
thein, house for meditation of monks, 114
the-mi-to, daughter, 91
thi, leaves, 132
thin, a grass, 48
thinbyu, mat woven from *thin,* 48
thingan, tree whose trunk is used for dug-out boats, 53
thitsi, wood oil, 52
thit-to, a kind of pear, 135
thok, mixed, 132
thugyi, headman or "elder persons" of a village, 87

ton-kyin-thi, shiver-sour-fruit, 135
to-sa-ya, dish of raw green vegetables, 130

u-bok-nay, duty day gathering in monastic rest house, 119
u-yin, garden, 68
upasin, a monk, 25

Waso, first month of Lent (July-August); every other year a double month, 79
wet, pig's flesh, 64
Wingaba, a maze, 167
winsa, possessed (by the spirit of one already dead), 30
wun-sa, lit. "food for the womb;" staple diet, 111

ya-khaing, type of check weave (for *longyis*) made in Arakan, 128
yamanè, coarse grained wood used for carving, 53
Yangon, lit. "end of strife," Rangoon, 165
Yan-gon-thu, Rangoon folk, 140
yaung-ma, sister-in-law, the stirrer of trouble; name given to wooden rice-stirrer, 55
yay-hnyi, slime moss, 129
yay-ngan, salt water, 135
Ye, town in Tenasserim, 23
yet-sa, linctus powder, 62
yi-sha, drawn up above the bosom, as a *longyi* is after bathing, 126
yun-it, lacquer box, 52
yway, adenanthera tree, 59
ywetyo, tree with edible fruit, 39

zat-pwè, traditional drama, 151
zaung-ya, a kind of fruit with five edges or blades, 132
zayat, rest house, 100
zi-byu-thi, Indian gooseberry, 138
zin-mè, geometric type of silk weave, 128
zun-chit, "spoon-scrape," as much of a fruit as a spoon will easily scrape, 93